KENT

Above The windmill, Sarre.

Following pages Picnickers enjoying the
spectacular view towards Romney Marsh from
Farthing Common on the edge of the Downs.

KENT

THE COUNTY IN COLOUR

Photographs

GREGORY HOLYOAKE

Text

JOHN E. VIGAR

THE DOVECOTE PRESS

This book is dedicated, with permission, to
Her Majesty Queen Elizabeth The Queen Mother,
to commemorate Her Majesty's 100th birthday, and
to mark the 21st Anniversary of The Queen Mother's Installation
as Lord Warden and Admiral of the Cinque Ports.

Tolhurst Farm near Smarden, a glorious example of timber-framed
vernacular architecture in the Weald.

First published in 2000 by The Dovecote Press Ltd
Stanbridge, Wimborne, Dorset BH21 4JD

ISBN 1 874336 75 X

Photographs © Gregory Holyoake 2000
Text © John E. Vigar 2000

Designed and produced by The Dovecote Press Ltd
Printed and bound in Singapore

A CIP catalogue record of this book is
available from the British Library

1 3 5 7 9 8 6 4 2

CONTENTS

KENT 7

DARTFORD AND THE NORTH 9

THE MEDWAY TOWNS AND THE SWALE 23

THE HOLIDAY COAST 39

HYTHE AND ROMNEY MARSH 63

CANTERBURY AND THE GARDEN OF ENGLAND 75

MAIDSTONE AND THE WEALD 93

TUNBRIDGE WELLS AND THE WEST 111

Acknowledgements 126

Index 127

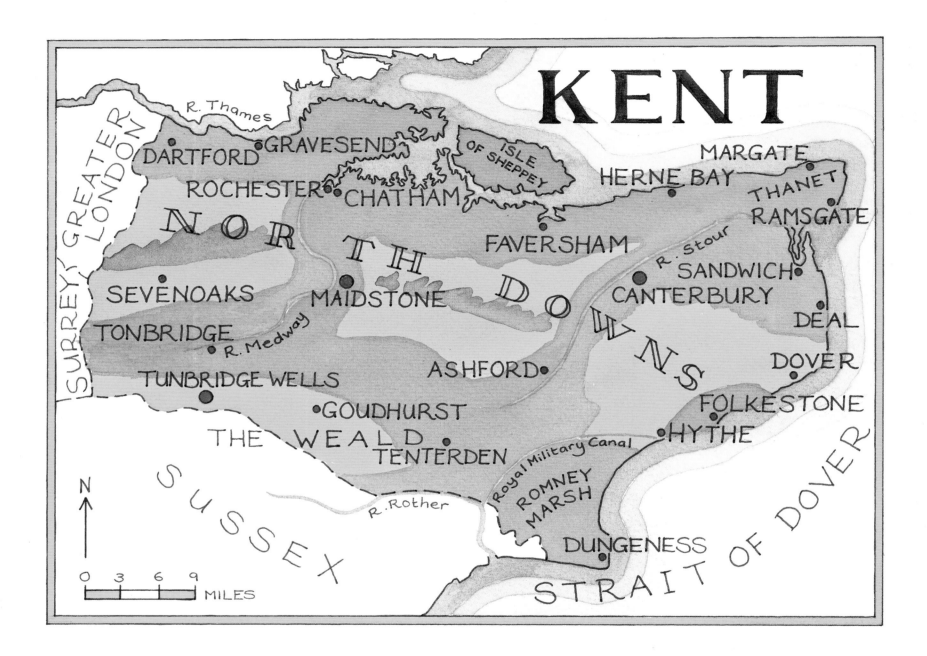

KENT

KENT is often called the 'Garden of England', yet it could equally be known as the 'Heel of Britain'. The heel is that essential part without which the body could not properly balance and in many ways Kent is – and has long been – Britain's balancing county. Without Kent and its very specific population the history of Britain would have been much different. Its people have both repelled and welcomed invaders; it is home to the world-wide Anglican church; it has long been the stepping stone to London and its white cliffs remain one of the most enduring images of our national pride and independence. It is the only member of the Heptarchy – the seven Kingdoms of Dark Age England – to have maintained its boundaries and identity: an achievement reflected in the county's motto '*Invicta*', or 'Unconquered'.

Kent's character has been formed by centuries of warfare. The Roman forts of Reculver and Richborough tell of its pioneer settlers; the Norman castles at Rochester and Dover were a statement of power in a newly conquered land; five castles on the south coast remind us that Kent stood in the Tudor front-line; Napoleon's threatened invasion caused great forts and a remarkable canal to be built; whilst the twentieth century has left gun emplacements and 'pill boxes' along the railways and rivers.

Unlike most English counties industrialisation in Kent was not predominantly of the eighteenth and nineteenth centuries. By the start of the Industrial Revolution, the Garden of England's industrial age was over. Four centuries ago the woodlands and ponds, the streams and tracks which today attract the walker were noisy, smoky and busy with people. Kent's half-timbered houses are the legacy of a golden age of industrialisation when iron was smelted, cloth woven and paper made in every available location. It was an age when agriculture took second place and only Kent's difficult terrain stopped the wholesale destruction of its ancient woodlands in the name of profit.

Yet whilst its historical importance is generally recognised, Kent is to many an unknown county. The traveller passes through it on the way to the Continent. But if that same traveller were to go to the deep narrow lanes above Wye, or the shingle expanses of the Romney Marshes, or the tranquil Darent Valley, few would think that the county's charms belonged to the past. Away from the main roads lies a countryside as rural as any, and a coastline still bleak and largely unspoilt. But Kent is not remote. Its proximity to the English Channel and to London has proved a great attraction over the centuries. Its medieval manors, Georgian mansions and Regency villas have long been home to those who wished to keep their distance from the capital, yet who still needed to keep their fingers on the pulse of the nation.

Kent is familiar to all those who love the work of Charles Dickens. The streets of Rochester and Broadstairs are alive with his characters and the north Kent marshes cry out for Magwitch, Pip and the creaking prison hulks. Other authors, too, have made their homes in this most enigmatic of counties. Russell Thorndike created his smuggling rector of Dymchurch, 'Dr Syn', in the flat landscape of Romney Marsh, whilst H. E. Bates placed his far more homely Larkin family in the agricultural heartland around Pluckley.

The early history of Christianity in Britain started in Kent. Introduced during Roman rule the Faith lingered amongst the native tribes of the Cantii until its widespread reintroduction under the Franks, encouraged by St Augustine and his followers. As a result of its early adoption by the Kentish royal family, the county boasts two early cathedrals; Canterbury founded in 597 and Rochester founded seven years later. The cathedrals encouraged the foundation of monasteries and parish churches, one of which, St Martin in Canterbury, has the undisputed claim of being the oldest parish church in England still in use. Medieval wealth, created by a strong agricultural and industrial economy, was mirrored in these religious buildings, the majority of which are constructed in Kent's native building materials of flint and ragstone.

No one in Kent is far from the influence of water. The English Channel is the world's busiest shipping lane and has been both friend and enemy to the people of Kent. Its width of twenty-two miles has protected them from invasion, but it has also been the reason for many of its ships being lost on the notorious Goodwin Sands. Its lighthouses bear witness to the perils its coastline continues to create. The north coast too, though less dangerous, has brought floods and destruction. It is only when we enter the Thames that the waters are calmer – but even here the brackish marshes dispensed plague and fever to those unwise enough to live near its banks. The River Medway, which cuts Kent in two and which traditionally divides its people into Men of Kent and Kentish Men, has been both boundary and lifeline, opening up the wealthy interior of the county to outside trade. The villages in its valley show agriculture and industry intertwined. In north Kent the Darent, that most overlooked of rivers, meanders through the Vale of Holmesdale with its watercress beds and meadows before cutting through the North Downs and emerging in Kent's most industrial landscape. In east Kent the Great and Little Stour rivers have been used for trade and communication. Even where there is no major waterway, it is rare to find even the tiniest stream that cannot boast a watermill or village pond.

Today the villages of Kent are more likely to house the commuter than those who spend their working lives in the county. The impact of the Channel Tunnel has been immense. The area round Ashford has witnessed a building boom without parallel in its history. The county's character, so dependant on its past, is changing once again. Yet despite such changes, Kent's coast and countryside, agriculture and industry, hill and vale are there to be enjoyed. Kent's diversity gives it strength and allows it to grow. History is as much about the present as it is about the past, and with such a heady brew of heritage, topography and architecture the Kent of today cannot fail to satisfy even the most discerning of palates.

JOHN E. VIGAR
Aylesford

DARTFORD AND THE NORTH

DARTFORD AND THE NORTH

The nineteenth and twentieth centuries were not kind to this corner of Kent, but with two great lines of communication, the River Thames and Roman Watling Street, cutting across it from west to east, it has always been something of a corridor. Chaucer's pilgrims rarely strayed from the main road. Similarly, the traveller by water – intent on reaching London in the shortest possible time – would only have paused when it was absolutely necessary. As a result only one major town, Gravesend, stands on the banks of the Thames, the others all turning their backs on the unhealthy marshes.

The railway also did north Kent few favours, encouraging the development of semi-urban communities that quickly became absorbed into Greater London. When in 1856 William Morris moved into his rural retreat, the 'Red House', he did so because the railway offered easy access to London.

The economy of the north was largely dependent on quarrying; providing employment, money for village clubs, the restoration of old churches and the opening of schools and libraries. Today, with many of the quarries closed, their communities

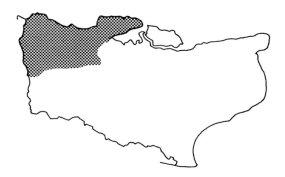

Previous page The statue of Pocahontas in St George's Churchyard, Gravesend. Pocahontas was a Cherokee Indian princess who saved the life of John Smith, one of the founders of Virginia. She later married another settler, John Rolfe, taking the name Rebecca. In 1616 she arrived in London with her husband and son and was presented at Court, much to the amusement of James I. A year later the family embarked for America, but Pocahontas died of pneumonia whilst her ship was moored at Gravesend.

Much of the town was destroyed by fire in 1727, and though the church was rebuilt her exact burial place remains unknown. The statue is a replica of one standing outside Jamestown Church in Virginia, where she was married.

Looking north from Swanscombe over the River Thames towards Tilbury and Grays in Essex. Now often known as the 'Thames Corridor', the industrial landscape behind the remnants of the old Swanscombe Marshes is a result of an enormous regeneration project that stretches from Dartford to Gravesend.

Swanscombe's industrial sprawl hides a distinguished past, for it was here in 1066 that William I met the people of Kent, giving back to them the ancient privileges that all English counties had been forced to surrender at the Conquest, an act which lead to the county's motto '*Invicta*', or 'Unconquered'.

The Queen Elizabeth II Bridge connects Kent and Essex and carries the M25 motorway around east London. The bridge was opened in 1991 and is the lowest permanent crossing over the River Thames (although there is a passenger ferry further downstream at Gravesend). The bridge brings traffic into Kent, whilst Essex-bound cars and lorries are carried north through two tunnels, built in 1963 and 1980. The road deck is 65 metres high, allowing even the tallest ships to pass underneath, whilst the 450 metre span between the two piers makes it one of the largest suspension bridges of its type in the world.

The view from the bridge is tremendous, both up and down river, as well as of the embryonic North Downs as they struggle for height from the river's edge. Although industrial parks and hotels cling to the approach roads, the bridge is a symbol of a new Kent, proud and graceful, modern yet based on tradition. Tactfully, the bridge doesn't claim to belong to Kent alone – it is a visible link of which both counties may be proud.

broken up and the schools, public houses and clubs a shadow of their former selves, it is easy to mourn the passing of a once vibrant way-of-life. In recent years new industries have arrived, typified by the opening in 1999 of Europe's largest retail and recreation centre, Bluewater. Abandoned industrial sites and forgotten churches are beginning to attract visitors. Old gravel pits are now home to over-wintering waders and wildfowl, whilst a greater appreciation of our past has encouraged those with an interest in Dickens, H.G. Wells, William Morris and Charles Darwin to visit the places they made famous.

What was once the market town of Bromley is now home to the many commuters who line its station platforms every morning. In some ways it is a parasite living off its proximity to London, but one which also feeds off those who live in rural Kent, just a couple of miles to the south, and to whom it is as important today as it was six centuries ago. It is only when you escape the magnetic pull of the railway that you appreciate just how quiet and remote some areas of north Kent can be. Knatts Valley – an unappealing name for one of the area's undiscovered gems, as well as the better known Darent Valley – could be two hundred miles from central London rather than twenty. Were it not for the shipping in the Thames and the industrialised Essex skyline in the distance, the north Kent marshes could easily be mistaken for one of the remotest places in Britain.

Bluewater, the largest shopping and leisure complex in Europe. Built in an abandoned chalk quarry not far from Swanscombe, the centre opened in 1999, bringing both employment and traffic problems to this corner of Kent. Its architecture is influenced by Kentish vernacular buildings – particularly noticeable in the conical roof vents which are based on oast house cowls. One of the three linked shopping malls has the course of the River Thames set in its marble floor. The centre is surrounded by fifty acres of landscaped parkland, which include nature reserves, six lakes and four kilometres of paths.

The mural in Bromley High Street to H.G. Wells. The writer H.G. Wells (1886-1946), who in a series of remarkable novels created what we now know as science-fiction, was born in the unlikely surroundings of a general store in Bromley High Street. His father was an unsuccessful shopkeeper, but an accomplished cricketer. H.G. Wells left Bromley when still young, but is today remembered by this enormous mural, which depicts scenes from his most famous book *The War of the Worlds*.

Down House, Downe. Originally a modest farmhouse, Down House is now internationally celebrated as the home of the naturalist Charles Darwin (1809-1892) who lived there from 1842 until his death. Shortly after returning from his five year voyage as naturalist on board HMS *Beagle*, Darwin looked around for a house close enough to the great institutions of London yet offering peace and fresh air. Despite worrying that he might turn into a 'Kentish hog' he chose the village of Downe, which even today preserves its feel of a rural community. He and his wife Emma enlarged the house as his family grew (they had ten children, of whom seven survived childhood). It was here that he wrote *On the Origin of Species* (1859), which completely reshaped modern thinking about evolution and is now widely regarded as one of the most influential of all books. Visitors to the house, which is owned by English Heritage, are able to see his study and many of his books, scientific instruments and collections.

Eltham Palace. This view shows the Great Hall built by King Edward IV in the 1470s. A popular royal hunting lodge since the early fourteenth century, the palace was used for tournaments and entertaining foreign visitors on their way to London. At its peak Eltham was larger than Hampton Court, but by the late Tudor period its popularity had waned in favour of the new palace at Greenwich and it became a farmhouse. It was rescued from ruin in the 1930s by the Courtauld family, who added Art Deco style wings – one of which is just visible on the right of this photograph – and it is now owned by English Heritage.

The Chinese Garage, alongside the busy Wickham roundabout, Beckenham. The garage dates from 1929 and was built in response to a national newspaper competition. There are flaming torches, carved Chinese symbols and an intricate bell turret: originally even the pumps were finished in Oriental black and gold. The Chinese Garage has been a Listed Building since 1994.

Above Printing silk at David Evans and Co. silk mill at Crayford. The company is the last of the old London silk printers and has been printing luxury silks on the banks of the River Cray since 1843. Their 'World of Silk' offers an introduction to the traditional craftsmanship and history of the material. In this photograph Bob Crane is demonstrating the screen printing process by producing silk squares for sale in the mill shop.

Hall Place, Bexley. A little corner of old England, Hall Place lies on the River Cray but within unhappily close earshot of the A2, which cuts it off from its former village. Hall Place was built in the 1540s by Sir Justinian Champneys, a former Lord Mayor of London, using stone plundered from monastic buildings combined with the ubiquitous local flint and red brick. After remaining a private house for over four centuries, it is now a local history museum whose gardens are a delight, especially in spring and early summer.

Red House, Bexleyheath. Surrounded by 1930s semi-detached housing and hidden behind a high brick wall, only a blue plaque tells the passer-by of the importance of this nineteenth century house. Designed by Philip Webb (1821-1915) in the then small hamlet of Upton in 1859 for his friend William Morris (1834-1896), it was Morris' first marital home and the ultimate Pre-Raphaelite building. It is hard to believe that when built it was surrounded by orchards, fields and copses, though a few apple and cherry trees still survive in the garden.

Despite being medieval in spirit, many architectural historians regard Red House as the first completely modern house to be built, inspiring both the Arts and Crafts Movement and twentieth-century modernist architecture. It was very much a house of its time – functional, solid, even homely. A simple three bedroom detached house with no airs or graces, it was designed as an L-shaped building of two storeys. The kitchen was much larger than normal at the time and its windows opened out onto the garden. For a while it was a hub round which the Pre-Raphaelite world revolved, but in 1865 worries about health and money forced Morris to move back to London.

Above Cobham Hall, Cobham. Set within parkland designed by Humphry Repton, Cobham Hall is today a girls' school. Formerly the seat of the Dukes of Lennox and Richmond and of the Earls of Darnley, this outstanding Elizabethan House is regularly open to the public.

Left The Leather Bottle, Cobham. It was here in *The Pickwick Papers* that Mr Pickwick 'entered a long low-roofed room furnished with a large number of high-backed leather-cushioned chairs, of fantastic shapes, and embellished with a great variety of old portraits and roughly-coloured prints of some antiquity' to find the lovelorn Tracy Tupman sitting down to a 'roast fowl, bacon, ale, etc. . .'.

Apart from the Dickens connection, which inevitably attracts most visitors, the pub's timber framing is unusual in not being painted black and white. The pub contains many Dickensian exhibits, but those visiting the village should also allow time for the parish church, which is celebrated for its brasses, and its delightful medieval almshouse, or College.

The 8th Earl of Darnley (as the Hon. Ivo Bligh) was a famous nineteenth century cricketer who in 1882 took an English team to Australia in hope of avenging an Australian victory at the Oval. After one match, an Australian, Florence Murphy, burnt a set of bails and presented the ashes to Ivo Bligh. The two of them later married, and Bligh returned to England with the 'Ashes' which he regarded as his personal property and kept in the house. According to folklore, the urn containing them was knocked over by a footman who subsequently topped them up with ash from the fireplace. On the death of her husband in 1927, the Countess of Darnley presented the urn to Lords, where it remains.

Owletts, Cobham. Seen in spring when a glorious display of snowdrops creates the perfect carpet, Owletts is a late seventeenth century brick house on the edge of the village. It was given to the National Trust in 1937 by the architect Sir Herbert Baker (1862-1946), whose yeoman family had lived in the house since 1780. Sir Herbert is best known for his collaboration with Sir Edwin Lutyens on New Delhi from 1912, but he was a close friend of Cecil Rhodes and spent much of his working life in South Africa, designing many of its great colonial buildings.

Nurstead Court, Nurstead, a working farmhouse in undeveloped countryside south of Gravesend. The left hand range is part of an impressive aisled hall house built in 1320, and is a precious and rare example of a late-medieval house. It was built when the width of a house was determined by the longest tree trunk that could be found, and when the only way of enlarging it was by building narrow passages, or aisles, to either side of the hall, thus widening the ground floor without extending the roof. Only a handful of such houses were built in England, and even though two thirds of the hall at Nurstead Court was demolished in the Regency period and replaced by a tall new range, Nurstead remains a place of pilgrimage for architectural historians.

Rounding a bend during the FIA International Historic Superprix at Brands Hatch. Familiar the world over as one of the homes of the British Grand Prix, Brands Hatch Circuit, on the Downs above Farningham, was founded in 1926. It was originally used for racing and pacemaking by cyclists, and the first track was laid out two years later. Brands can claim a history of 'firsts' – from the first motorcycle race to be screened by the BBC in 1947 to the erection of the first permanent grandstand to be built at a British race track in 1955.

The River Thames at Gravesend. Originally a port, then a resort, and now a major commercial centre, Gravesend was formerly famous for its shrimping industry: until the nineteenth century its inhabitants were affectionately known as 'shrimpies'. A foot ferry runs across the river here to Tilbury in Essex and the Port of London Authority commences its control of the river at this point. The name Gravesend comes from Grove's End, or the 'place where the trees meet the river'. In 1865 General Gordon, later to lose his life at Khartoum, supervised the construction of Gravesend's coastal defences, and a statue to his memory has been erected near his former home.

Above A summer's day on the River Darent at Farningham. The Lion Hotel has been a favourite watering hole for over two centuries, starting life as a coaching inn on the main London to Dover road. Its architecture is surprisingly urban for a tiny village, with bow windows and dainty ironwork. To the right is a mock bridge of three arches supposedly built to stop cattle straying upstream from the nearby meadows, but more likely intended as an ornamental feature for the inn's pleasure gardens.

Right Eynsford's ford and seventeenth century stone bridge. In contrast to Farningham's peaceful riverside, that at neighbouring Eynsford often gets over-crowded. The village's popularity dates back to the early days of motoring when the Darent Valley was a reasonable drive from south-east London. Four generations later, a visit to Eynsford is an established part of many family's excursions.

Just a mile away, and often overlooked, is Lullingstone, which boasts the most famous Roman villa in Kent, a Norman church and Tudor castle.

Cooling Castle. The massive gatehouse of Cooling Castle seems out of place in the open landscape leading onto the Hoo peninsula. There is no town to protect, no bridge or stately home, and the castle was built by Sir John de Cobham in 1381 as a reminder to French raiders of the danger of sailing too far up the Thames. It was attacked by Sir Thomas Wyatt during his brief rebellion of 1544 against the marriage of Queen Mary to Philip of Spain and was badly damaged. In a county containing castles as historically important as Dover and Rochester, Cooling remains little more than an impressive curiosity.

Dode Church. This atmospheric church is all that remains of a village whose inhabitants died during the Black Death of 1348. The twelfth century church would have served the small agricultural community who farmed this dry valley on the top of the North Downs. It gradually fell into disrepair, becoming an object of curiosity for antiquarians who had few other tangible examples of deserted medieval villages in Kent. It was restored in the early twentieth century, and is now privately owned. The interior reflects a setting that might have been found in many of our churches seven hundred years ago, with candlelight, straw on the floor, and a sense of almost theatrical medieval spectacle.

Pip's Graves, St James Church, Cooling. Beautifully cared for by The Churches Conservation Trust, St James's receives more visitors than most medieval churches in this part of Kent. The reason is simple. It is the setting for the dramatic opening scene in *Great Expectations* where the young Pip is approached by the escaped convict Magwitch whilst looking at his family tombstones. Charles Dickens (1812-1870), whose house at Gad's Hill is only a few miles across the open countryside, must have often visited the church, gaining the idea for the novel's opening scene from these tiny graves, each representing a member of the Comport family: though in the novel Dickens reduced their number from thirteen to five rather than strain his readers' credulity. A familiar sight in Kent churchyards, it is unusual to find such a large grouping of 'bodystones' as this.

The High Street, Upnor, with the River Medway beyond. Surprisingly few villages and towns are to be found on the estuaries of the Thames or Medway, mainly because so much of it is bleak and inhospitable marshland. Gravesend is the major exception, occupying a central position on Kent's Thameside shore. To the east of Gravesend, on the western bank of the Medway, lies Upnor, an unassuming maritime village that grew up in the shadow of a castle built by Elizabeth I in 1559 to protect the Royal Dockyard opposite. It was at the end of this street in 1667 that the Dutch navy broke the boom guarding the English fleet, burnt four ships, and towed away the 80-gun *Royal Charles*, the largest ship in the fleet, all under the noses of Upnor Castle's under-munitioned and inefficient gunners.

THE MEDWAY TOWNS
AND THE SWALE

THE MEDWAY TOWNS
AND THE SWALE

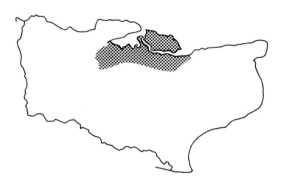

THE Medway Towns of Strood, Rochester, Chatham and Gillingham boast a long and illustrious history. The Royal Dockyard at Chatham was established in the sixteenth century and is now the site of the World Naval Base. Serviced by men from Gillingham and the surrounding villages until its closure in 1984, it was traditionally the area's major employer. The historic centre of Medway is Rochester, which grew up in the shadow of its Norman castle and cathedral, but which for much of its history took second place to Chatham and its Dockyard. The more picturesque aspects of its heritage have recently helped to forge a new identity. It is the town where Charles Dickens reigns supreme and where astute shopkeepers have long taken advantage of his fame by adding the name of one his characters to their own. The once independent towns of Strood and Gillingham are now part of the same unitary authority as Rochester and Chatham and cannot compete with their all too modest attractions. Yet the four combine to form the largest single conurbation in Kent.

To the east of the Medway Towns lies the enigmatic and slightly romantic Isle of Sheppey, which takes its name from the sheep which still graze there. Sheppey is a microcosm of Kent: its marshland rising to tall cliffs, its history ranging from the Romans via the Saxon Kentish royal family and early monasticism to another Naval Dockyard and heavy twentieth century industry. It is linked to the mainland by just one bridge and can still feel remote, even on a summer's day when it fills with visitors. Sheppey also incorporates the two forgotten islands of Elmley and Harty: surely the least altered landscapes to be found in north Kent? The water which separates the Island from the mainland is known as the Swale, Old English for a 'swirling river'.

Thanks to its location between Watling Street and the head of a small creek off the River Swale, Faversham is one of the most atmospheric towns in the county. King Stephen founded its abbey and it grew into a major medieval town. An early grammar school, brewery and gunpowder works add to its colourful history, whilst its Heritage Centre has been the model for many others across the country.

Inland from the rivers and coastline, the slope northwards from the crest of the Downs provides the ideal soil and climate for fruit farming, recorded in these villages for the past seven hundred years. The orchards are best visited during blossom time, but the unspoilt countryside in this part of Kent is a delight throughout the year. The national collection of fruit trees, the Brogdale Trust, continues to flourish just outside Faversham. Were it not for the M2, which was built before motorway landscaping was thought necessary, this part of north Kent would be amongst the most picturesque in the county. Even so, it is still possible to get lost on the single track lanes that criss-cross the dry valleys linking the villages.

Previous page A Thames barge on the River Swale.

Opposite page top Looking at the Medway down Chatham Reach. The river is very wide at this point and forms a natural harbour. Chatham town centre is to the right, with Rochester off to the left. The World Naval Base and Historic Dockyard are in the distance on the right. The narrow streets at the bottom of the picture were built around small piers, giving sailors as short a walk as possible when returning to their ships after a night in the many inns that still flourish in this part of the High Street.

Opposite page bottom The M2 Medway Bridge. The bridge's graceful 500 feet span dominates the Medway Valley where the river cuts through the North Downs escarpment.

The Norman keep of Rochester Castle. Although the castle is now a ruin, its strategic position on a bend overlooking the Medway becomes all too obvious once you've climbed on to its battlements. The site was originally occupied by a Roman fort, then by the Saxon castle that gave the town its name, *Hrofe Caestre*. Its Norman replacement was built in about 1080 by Bishop Gundulph, and the keep – whose ragstone walls are 12 feet thick – in the early twelfth century by William de Corbeuil, then Archbishop of Canterbury.

During the Baron's War against King John in 1215, the south-east tower was undermined in an attempt to drive out the rebel garrison. The latest innovations in defensive design were incorporated into the repairs, hence a rounded corner on a building that had previously been completely square.

The west front of the Cathedral Church of Christ and the Blessed Virgin Mary, Rochester. The see was founded by St Augustine in 604, who built a small stone cathedral, of which traces survive under the nave floor. The Saxon building was sacked by the Vikings, and Bishop Gundulph started work on the present cathedral shortly after the Norman Conquest. Time has not been kind to the original building. It has been sacked, damaged by fire, and the victim of vandalism; whilst nineteenth century 'restoration' was often heavy-handed and out-of-keeping. Despite its history, or perhaps because of it, the result is a building that mixes styles from virtually every period of English architecture (from the Lady Chapel it is possible to see work of every century from the eleventh to the twenty-first), and it is this stylistic jumble that makes the building architecturally such a delight.

Above Two Post Alley, Rochester. One of many medieval alleyways which run from the High Street, Two Post Alley is aptly named and frames a tantalising glimpse of the Norman keep.

Chertsey's Gate in Rochester High Street. Formerly the boundary between City and Monastery, this solid old gateway adds great character to the city. The horizontal banding of alternate stone and flint is a local characteristic and may be seen in several other buildings in the area. The gateway dates from the fourteenth century, and is one of three of this date to survive in the city, although the weatherboarded top is much later. It gets its unofficial name of Jasper's Gate from the character of John Jasper, the choirmaster who lived in the house in Dickens' unfinished novel *The Mystery of Edwin Drood*.

Above Characters from *Oliver Twist* taking part in the Rochester Dickens Festival (there's a Fagin, Bill Sikes, Nancy and Bet). Twice a year Rochester pays homage to its most famous nineteenth century resident, Charles Dickens. Many of the buildings and characters that Dickens used in his stories gained inspiration in the city that he loved, particularly in *Great Expectations, The Mystery of Edwin Drood*, and *Pickwick Papers*. In *Pickwick* Mr Jingle speaks of it as a 'fine place. . . glorious pile – frowning walls – tottering arches – dark nooks – crumbling staircases. . .', before describing its inhabitants as 'all sorts of old fellows, with great red faces, and broken noses. . .' .

Above The Six Poor Travellers House, Rochester. This rare example of a travellers hostel was founded by Richard Watts, one of the city's Elizabethan mayors and MPs. It provided one night's accommodation for six poor travellers, 'not being rogues or proctors', who each was given a bedroom with a fireplace and a small sum of money to set them on their journey. The house was used for its original purpose until 1940 when wartime regulations meant that it had to close. Whilst the interior is relatively unchanged from its Elizabethan origins, the High Street frontage is a rebuilding of 1771, carried out (unusually for Rochester where brick was fashionable) in Portland limestone.

Left The *Kingswear Castle* below Rochester Castle. The coal-fired paddle steamer was built in 1924 for service on the River Dart in Devon. Withdrawn from service in 1965 she was restored under the auspices of the Paddle Steamer Preservation Society and is now based in the World Naval Base at Chatham's Historic Dockyard. In the summer regular services are operated on the Medway, as well as special sailings to London and Essex.

Above The figurehead from HMS *Wellesley* which stands near the main entrance to Chatham Historic Dockyard. The *Wellesley* was launched in 1815 as a third-rate ship of 74 guns, and was named after the Marquis of Wellesley, Governor General of India during the Napoleonic Wars and brother of the 1st Duke of Wellington. The colourful figurehead, however, must surely be of the Duke, for the *Wellesley* was launched in the year of his most famous victory, Waterloo.

Left Navy Day at the World Naval Base. An annual event whilst the Navy were in occupation this event was re-established in 1999 with the temporary arrival of many British and foreign ships. The first ships to be built in Chatham were launched in the late sixteenth century following Elizabeth I's founding of the dockyard. Under the Stuarts it was enlarged to become the main naval base in the country, and shipbuilding reached its peak at about the time of the construction of HMS *Victory* in 1765. A permanent exhibition charting the construction of a warship is the most popular attraction in the Historic Dockyard, which is the most perfectly preserved Georgian Dockyard in the world.

The Kingsferry Bridge linking Kent and the Isle of Sheppey. The bridge was opened in 1960, and its four concrete pillars give it the look of an upturned table, a similarity even more pronounced when the bridge is raised. Although it causes severe traffic delays at peak times this bridge, which also carries the railway between Sittingbourne and Sheerness, is a much loved feature of the Swale riverscape.

Queenborough Creek. Queenborough is best described as a 'decayed port'. It was founded in the fourteenth century to serve a castle built by Edward III to protect the Swale estuary, and still retains its medieval street plan. The town is named after Edward III's queen, Philippa of Hainault.

When nearby Sheerness Dockyard was laid out by Samuel Pepys in the 1660s Queenborough became a residential town for naval officers, leading to much refronting and rebuilding of houses.

The castle was finally demolished during the construction of the railway, and Queenborough became an industrial town – from which it has yet to fully recover.

Above The Ferry House Inn, Harty, stands on the site of a much earlier inn. It was built to serve travellers using a now vanished ferry across the Swale at the eastern end of the Isle of Sheppey, and despite its isolation is still remarkably popular.

Below left Harty church. The remotest church in Kent, Harty has never enjoyed the protection of a village. It continues to serve a small and scattered farming community. Dedicated to St Thomas the Apostle, it is still lit by oil lamps and candles and contains a fine fifteenth century image niche and a world famous fourteenth century Flemish chest carved with a scene of two jousting knights. A modern stained glass window depicts the sheep which made the island famous.

Below Newington Church. A typical view across the open landscapes of north Kent not far from the Swale.

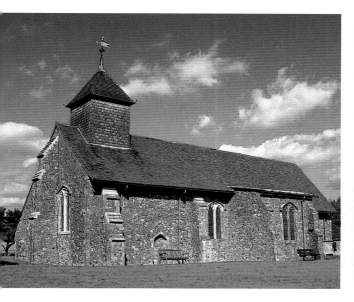

Above The Plough Inn, Stalisfield, stands high on a plateau where the North Downs escarpment gradually dips to meet the River Swale. Unknown even to many locals, it embodies the best traditions of the village inn, playing a central role in the social life of the surrounding rural community.

Right Cherry pickers at Teynham. In 1376 the Manor of Teynham sent cherries to the Archbishop of Canterbury, a gift that is also the first known mention of cherries being grown in England. A hundred and fifty years later, Richard Harris, fruitier to Henry VIII, replanted a hundred acres with imported stock, from which most Kentish cherry orchards later developed. Note the use of the traditional tapering ladders that were designed to slip easily between the dense branches.

Calico House, Newnham. The village is one of the most picturesque in north Kent, comprising a traditional pub, thirteenth century church and a wide variety of domestic architecture. Calico House began life as a medieval hall house. In the early eighteenth century tulips were painted on the first floor walls, making it a rare example in Kent of external applied decoration.

The Light Railway at Sittingbourne. A former industrial line, the 2ft 6in gauge Sittingbourne and Kemsley Light Railway now carries passengers across the marshland on a two mile journey to Kemsley Down.

Oare Marshes. A desolated but endearing area of marshland that at first glance appears to be a completely natural environment, but which in reality is intensively managed to protect its wildlife habitats. Once a thriving route from the mainland to Harty Ferry, and later the site of a Victorian Gun Cotton Factory, the marsh is gradually being returned to its natural state. Following severe flooding in 1953 a new sea wall was built, which led to the former salt marshes becoming freshwater and thus suitable for grazing stock. The sea wall gives magnificent views over the Swale to the southern shore of the Isle of Sheppey.

Above Abbey Street, Faversham, is the most attractive in a town containing a large concentration of listed buildings. A preservation scheme was initiated in the 1960s, creating a townscape uncluttered by overhead wires and unsympathetic street furniture. The houses shown here are mostly timber-framed, with later fronts in plaster, hung tile or brick, relieved by the occasional facade of mathematical tile much loved in the eighteenth century as a means of bringing houses up to date without having to lose too much ground.

Left Barges and an old oyster warehouse at Faversham Creek, which is still a working harbour. The town was prosperous from early in the Middle Ages (the medieval weigh-house still stands), though the continual silting up of the channel joining it to the Swale meant that only shallow draught vessels could use the harbour. In 1558 a sluice was built at the head of the Creek. Water collected at high tide was released at low tide to keep the channel clear. Following nineteenth century improvements even larger ships were able to dock, leading to the Victorian buildings that survive today.

Right The Guildhall, Faversham. The Guildhall was built in 1574 as a Market Hall and remains the focus of the town centre, with stalls regularly gathering round its octagonal oak columns. Following a fire in 1814 the upper floor and tower were rebuilt and their clean Regency lines contrast well with the medieval timber-framed buildings that surround it. The upper floor is now the Magistrate's Court. Like many of the town's buildings, the Guildhall is open on set dates during the summer under the long-running Open House Scheme.

Below Faversham's ornate town pump is linked to a well named after Saint Crispin, patron saint of shoemakers, who is traditionally believed to have sheltered here after fleeing from Rome in the third century. Its rather mundane purpose was to wash fish on market days. Local tradition insists that if pumped on Christmas Day it dispenses beer from the nearby brewery!

Arden's House, Faversham. The only major surviving part of Faversham Abbey founded by King Stephen in 1147, and of which it formed the outer gateway, the building was converted to a private house immediately after the Dissolution by Thomas Arden, later Faversham's mayor. Although stone-built and with timber upper storeys, it would be little more than a picturesque historic building had it not been for Arden's murder here in February 1551 by his wife Alice and her lover. Alice was burnt to death at Canterbury a month after the murder, whilst her lover was hanged at Smithfield. The story of the murder, published as a play as early as 1592 under the title of *Arden of Faversham,* and which until recently was thought to be written by either Shakespeare or Marlowe, is still regularly performed, bringing a certain notoriety to this charming house.

Above The Hop Doorway, Faversham. The town is the home of the independent brewers, Shepherd Neame, whose brewery was established in 1698 to take advantage of a series of clear springs in the vicinity. This doorway to the Brewery offices in Court Street, which dates from 1869, displays a colourful frieze of hop bines showing the cones, or flowers, which are used in the brewing process.

THE HOLIDAY COAST

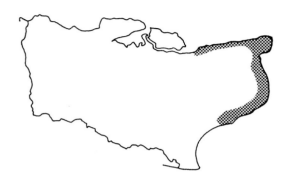

WHILST Kent cannot lay claim to have invented the seaside holiday, its coastal towns have attracted visitors for so long that their names are part of our nation's collective childhood. Margate started the ball rolling in the 1730s. Within fifty years it was a major resort, offering accommodation, entertainment and the chance to indulge the new-fangled habit of 'sea-bathing'.

Thanet's resorts started as inland settlements. Their Norman churches, still to be found in villages whose character has little to do with the sea, are a legacy of the island's medieval wealth. The Romans first farmed Thanet, a tradition continuing into the present. Abruptly meeting twentieth century sprawl, acres of cauliflowers and other crops create an often desolate welcome. Thanet's circuitous roads make exploration difficult, and it is easy to become lost before emerging triumphant at the North Foreland Lighthouse. South of Pegwell Bay's mudflats the fairways of the Royal St George's Links stretch over land reclaimed from the River Wantsum, which once divided the Isle of Thanet from mainland Kent. It is a birdwatcher and walker's paradise, with the medieval port of Sandwich nearby if it gets too blowy.

The wind once provided Deal's renowned boatmen with a living, for in virtually all weathers it was they who supplied the ships anchored in the Downs, who served as pilots and salvage crews. Not all Kent's resorts have kept their character. Dover, just eight miles down the coast, is now an industrial sprawl and overnight stop for travellers bound for the Continent. Wartime damage and a road system that divides the town

Previous page The colourful helter-skelter at the Rotunda Amusement Park on Folkestone Beach.

Beach huts at Whitstable. A traditional Kentish beach scene of pebbles, open skies and a regiment of beach huts. Whitstable is a shy, forgotten place on the exposed north Kent coast. Part fishing port, seaside resort and retirement town, it has recently become increasingly cosmopolitan and fashionable. Most of the town is built behind a tall sea wall and were it not for the myriad of alleyways that run from the High Street, the visitor could be forgiven for not realising they were on the coast at all.

A plate of Whitstable oysters. In recent years Whitstable has seen a resurgence of an industry that dates back at least as early as 1182, when King Stephen gave a license to the Faversham Oyster Company, making it the oldest limited company in the world.

Whitstable's beds are in three areas, which extend from the low water mark two miles out to sea, on sea bed relinquished by George III. The only company still farming the native oyster is the Seasalter and Ham Oyster Company, who as well as sowing spats, or baby oysters, onto their beds at Whitstable, supply spats for other oyster farms throughout Britain. At any one time, the company has fourteen million oysters fattening on its beds. There are two main varieties, the Pacific Oyster, which can be eaten all the year round, and the English native, which is only served when there is an 'r' in the month. The days when oysters were poor man's fare is long over, but the waters at Reeves Bay are still traditionally blessed in July at the start of the season and the town's oyster bars do a roaring trade when the native oyster is in season.

from its seafront add to its woes. But its past makes up for its present. A painted Roman villa, a clifftop Roman lighthouse, Saxon church, Norman castle, Napoleonic fortifications, wartime bunkers . . . the list could easily lengthen.

Folkestone was developed in the late nineteenth century by the Earl of Radnor as an up-market resort. Its famous clifftop walk, The Leas, creates an area of great character, but the town never quite matches up to expectations – its working harbour and holiday hotels striking an uneasy balance. Instead, travel west to Sandgate, a one-street town with dramatic coastal views, colour-washed houses and a bustling atmosphere. Its beach huts, the faded grandeur of its once elegant houses, and the modern flats that prove it to be an evolving community, somehow work together to produce a place of great charm. Hythe is a lovely town at the foot of a cliff, but it has lost its sea. Tiny alleys lead uphill to the magnificent church in whose churchyard rests Lionel Lukin, the inventor of the lifeboat. But the largest stretch of water near the town centre is the Royal Military Canal, set into a deep cutting. The sea itself is a long trudge, but once there miles of shingle stretch as far as the eye can see, punctuated by the Martello Towers built to stop Napoleon.

Kent's holiday towns have been forced to change to meet the demands of modern visitors. Those reliant on tourism have had to make major investment to compete with the more picturesque parts of England. Yet this practice does succeed; Herne Bay, a few years ago run down and forgotten, now enjoys greater popularity than in its nineteenth century heyday. Deal and Sandgate have real character, and for those looking for unspoilt countryside there are miles of protected coastline with cliffs and saltmarshes. With three quarters of the county's boundary formed by coast and estuary it is surprising that its influence does not stretch further inland. Perhaps that is why we like it. It offers an escape and reinforces our sense of individualism.

Above The Old Neptune Inn at Whitstable is a white weatherboarded pub that stands right on the beach. It was once the haunt of smugglers who, in addition to their usual activities, are supposed to have lined their pockets still further by repatriating French prisoners-of-war during the Napoleonic Wars.

Opposite page top Sunset from Whitstable beach. The north Kent coast is famous for its sunsets over the sea, which are an unusual occurrence in eastern England.

Opposite page bottom The seafront, Herne Bay. Herne Bay is a planned nineteenth century resort that failed to live up to its promise. Although it was laid out on a grand scale and provided with a pier, the town never became the fashionable resort intended by its developers. Decay was followed by a more recent renaissance, which has included a leisure complex, library and museum, as well as a seaside sculpture trail. The town's best-known landmark is its clock tower which, when built in 1837, was the tallest free standing clock tower in the world.

Left Reculver Towers. The stark ruined church of St Mary, Reculver, marks one of the landmark sites in Kent history. It was here that King Ethelbert (died 616) was converted to Christianity, an event marked by the erection of a standing cross and shortly afterwards by a church to house it. Much of the church was built with stone robbed from the abandoned Roman fort that stood nearby. First the fort, then the church, stood on a promontory, or tip, of mainland Kent that faced eastwards across the Wantsum Channel towards the Isle of Thanet. By the fourteenth century the channel had silted up and Thanet today is an island in name only. Reculver church remained in use until 1809, when it was partially demolished by its parson in favour of a new church in a more convenient location inland. Only the thirteenth century west towers were left standing, thanks to the Board of Trinity House, who recognised their importance as a landmark to mariners, and massive sea defences now protect the towers from further damage.

Margate's Tudor House Museum. Hidden behind later seafront developments is this charming timber-framed house. Rare in Thanet, where flint is the most common building material, the Tudor House is a twentieth century reconstruction of a farmhouse that once stood on the site.

Taking a spin at Dreamland in Margate, Kent's oldest amusement park.

Originally a late Victorian pleasure park developed by Lord George Sangar, it included a music hall, waxworks, roller-skating rink, ornamental gardens, and fairground. The star of Sangar's Circus was 'Emperor', a lion trained to walk along two tightropes over a lake, which he one night fell into when startled by fireworks!

After the First World War, at a time when Margate was popularly known for its 'landladies, aspidistras, fish and chips, and concert parties on the sand', the complex was extended by Henry Isle, a local celebrity, acquiring its present name, as well as a ballroom and 'super' cinema (complete with Compton organ). Dreamland's heyday was immediately after the Second World War, when it was a popular night out for local factory girls dating American G.I.s stationed at R.A.F. Manston.

The view from the stage of the Theatre Royal, Margate.

Margate's rise began in the mid eighteenth century, though its first visitors preferred to stay inland in a sheltered valley within walking distance of the sea. Bathing machines arrived in 1753, and in 1769 Cecil Square was laid out to provide the resort with a social focus. In one corner, behind a plain facade, stands England's second oldest theatre, which opened in 1787 and whose lights remain undimmed.

The interior of the theatre is delightful. The horseshoe-shaped galleries are exquisitely carved with cherubs and swags of flowers.

The chalk stack at Botany Bay. The most atmospheric of Thanet's beaches, Botany Bay is a sandy north-facing cove enclosed by tall cliffs. The cliffs are an important nature reserve, whose rare coastal flora and fauna flourish undisturbed by the hundreds of holidaymakers who visit the cove. 'Botany Bay' is a common eighteenth century name for a remote place, and one can imagine early visitors to Margate riding out to the cove to take the salt air and feeling as if on the edge of the world. Smugglers' legends abound, and none more so than the infamous 'Battle of Botany Bay' of 1769 led by local smuggler Joss Snelling, in which ten smugglers and an excise officer were killed.

The North Foreland Lighthouse. Until its automation in 1999 this was the last manned lighthouse on the British mainland. Built in the late seventeenth century of flint and brick which was later rendered, the 85 feet high octagonal lighthouse is a familiar landmark to those exploring Kent's most easterly coastal road between Margate and Broadstairs. It was described by Charles Dickens, who lived nearby, as 'a severe parsonic light, which reproves the young and giddy floaters, and stares grimly out to sea'.

Viking Bay, Broadstairs, the most picturesque of all Kent beaches. The town stands high on the cliff above and has the character of an inland town, whilst the beach is reached by a steep narrow road which emerges at the tiny harbour. Though often crowded in summer, Broadstairs has managed to preserve its character. Visible on the top of the hill are charming rows of fishermen's and smuggler's cottages, beloved of many nineteenth century writers and artists, including Wilkie Collins and J.M.W. Turner.

Bleak House, Broadstairs. The clifftop holiday home of the author Charles Dickens overlooks the harbour below. The building was much enlarged by a later owner, but the wing facing the sea, to the right of this picture, is the part which Dickens knew and loved. Dickens first came to Broadstairs in 1837, when the house was known as Fort House, working on *Pickwick Papers* at a house in the High Street. Bleak House was where he finished *David Copperfield* and started work on *Bleak House*, after which the house was later renamed. An annual Dickens Festival has been held in Broadstairs each June since 1937 and the town still enjoys its Dickensian celebrations.

Above Royal Harbour, Ramsgate. The harbour took advantage of the port of Sandwich's decline as a result of the silting up of the River Stour, growing prosperous on trade with both the Baltic and the East. It still bustles, with pleasure craft as well as commercial traffic filling its quays. The cliffs rising above the harbour are faced with an artificial stone, 'Pulhamite', which was added early in the last century to make the stark chalk more attractive, and a rocky glen of the same material leads up to Wellington Crescent. Many of the town's street names reflect the late eighteenth and early nineteenth century periods in which they were laid out.

Above right The Clock House, Ramsgate. The harbour buildings were designed by John Shaw in the early nineteenth century. There is a superb maritime museum housed in the Clock House of 1815 whilst a nearby obelisk commemorates the embarkation of George IV for Hanover in 1820.

Right Half-timbered houses at Ramsgate Model Village on the West Cliff.

No period in Kent's history has more deeply etched itself in the national conscious than the Battle of Britain, much of which was fought in the skies over the county during the summer of 1940. The part played by Kent's front-line fighter bases (Biggin Hill, Hawkinge, Manston, West Malling) led to it being christened 'Hell's', or 'Hellfire', 'Corner', and at Manston, the closest wartime airfield to the coast, a memorial building has been opened to house both a Spitfire and Hurricane. This Spitfire, registration TB752, is one of the few surviving aircraft of its type to have seen active wartime service. The Museum is open throughout the year.

A perhaps more moving memorial is the official Battle of Britain Memorial, at Capel-le-Ferne on the cliffs north of Folkestone. It was unveiled in 1993 by Her Majesty Queen Elizabeth the Queen Mother as a permanent tribute to the young fighter pilots whose courage prevented the Germans obtaining air supremacy over the Channel, in which 426 of them lost their lives.

The battle began in July with attacks on British shipping. A month later, the *Luftwaffe* turned its attention to the airfields of the south-east, using fleets of bombers protected by fighters, a policy it abandoned as their losses mounted. The bombing of London that followed was a tacit admission that Britain would not be brought down by military conquest. The Germans made one final but ineffective effort to destroy Fighter Command on September 15th, after which the changes to both tide and moon made invasion impossible. German losses during the battle totalled 1,733 planes, whilst the British lost 915.

The venerable abbey at Minster. The abbey was founded in 669 by King Egbert to make amends for the murder of two young princes who might otherwise have been rival claimants to his Kentish throne. According to tradition, the abbey's boundaries were decided by the flight of a tame deer belonging to Ermenburga, the princes' sister and its first abbess.

The monastery's most famous abbess was St Mildred, who after being miraculously preserved from certain death in a French oven became Kent's most popular early saint, and whose shrine was an important place of pilgrimage until her remains were moved to St Augustine's Abbey in Canterbury by King Canute in the eleventh century. The buildings at Minster subsequently became a working farm until its re-establishment as a Benedictine nunnery in 1937. The surviving buildings, of flint with stone dressings, are in a quiet and pretty corner of this sprawling village, and the nuns welcome visitors at advertised times.

The tall gaunt walls of Richborough Castle and a series of earthen banks and ditches are all that remain of *Rutupiae*, once the gateway to Roman Britain and still the finest Roman monument in the south. It was here that the Emperor Claudius landed in 43 AD with a force of 40,000 men to begin the conquest of Britain. A fortified bridgehead was constructed in the wake of the landings, whilst a triumphal arch in the centre of the site formed a symbolic entrance to this far-flung corner of the Empire.

Rutupiae soon grew into a major military headquarters, as well as an administrative centre, complete with its own mint, granaries and villas. It stood on the banks of the Wantsum Channel, along which the galleys sailed from the open sea, although by medieval times the Channel had silted up, making it landlocked. In the third century, with Rome threatened and the first Saxon raiders beginning to land in Britain, a stone fort (known as a Saxon Shore fort) was built at Richborough, and it is the remains of that fort that survive today. The foundations of a small Saxon church prove that the site continued to be occupied even after the departure of the Romans.

The view from St Clement's Church, Sandwich, towards the flat lands of what once was the Wantsum Channel, separating the Isle of Thanet from the mainland. Sandwich is now two miles inland, and it is hard to believe that the town was once England's premier port.

Decline seemed inevitable when its harbour started silting up in about 1500. Fifty years later the medieval wool merchants were replaced by Protestant weavers from the Low Countries, forced to flee religious persecution. Some continued weaving, particularly flannel and serge, whilst others turned to market gardening in this fertile valley of the Stour. But their legacy is most obvious in the town's architecture: note the pantiles, or curved red roof tiles, brought originally as ship's ballast and now such a characteristic feature of Sandwich. The church in the centre is St Peter's, whose onion-shaped dome was added following storm damage in the 1660s.

The Barbican toll bridge, Sandwich. Sandwich is one of the original Cinque Ports and has the distinction of having more listed buildings per head of population than any other place in the country. The Barbican, which was built in the reign of Henry VIII, has chequerwork walling and is entered via the former toll bridge across the River Stour. Tolls were last imposed here in 1977, and a board on the wall continues to list the charges. The quay here is still busy, whilst nearby Strand Street boasts the longest continuous run of timber-framed buildings in England.

Left The Time Ball Tower Museum, Deal. A notable local landmark, the Time Ball Tower was built as a semaphore station in about 1820 to assist in the pursuit of smugglers by the revenue service. In 1855 the tower was equipped with a 'time ball', which was raised to the top of a mast and dropped daily at 1 pm to provide shipping in the Downs with an accurate time check, so that ships' chronometers could be set to determine their longitude. The signal was sent from the Royal Observatory at Greenwich by telegraph down the railway lines, and a similar device still survives at Greenwich today. Because the signal's accuracy was vital to naval navigation an elaborate back-up system was in place should the ball have fallen at the wrong time! The Tower is now a museum and although the 'time ball' is no longer connected to the Royal Observatory, it is still raised for the benefit of visitors.

Above Deal seafront from its 1000 feet long pier (opened in 1957 and the most recent to be built in Britain). The original settlement lies on high ground away from the sea, but the construction of Deal, Sandown and Walmer castles by Henry VIII to protect the Downs – the safe if confusingly named anchorage between the mainland and the Goodwin Sands – lead to the growth of a new town on the shore.

Deal is a happy and atmospheric town which really comprises three long parallel streets linked by a network of narrow interconnecting alleys. Middle Street was the first Conservation area in Kent, and is rich in eighteenth and nineteenth century brick-built houses.

A day trip by Hovercraft to the Goodwin Sands. Supposedly named after Earl Godwin, father of the Harold who fell at Hastings, the Sands lie three-and-a-half-miles off the Kent coast and are as notorious a ship's graveyard as any in the Channel. They stretch for twelve miles and are five miles wide at their broadest, and their shifting soft sands mean that once grounded in a storm wooden sailing ships were literally cracked open by the waves.

Shakespeare's description of them as a place 'where the carcasses of many a tall ship lie buried' is no exaggeration. 1,200 sailors lost their lives on the Sands during the 'Great Storm' of 1703. As recently as 1954 the South Goodwins lightship parted her riding cable and was swept onto the Sands with the loss of all hands.

Occasional trips in aid of charity are run by Hovercraft to the Sands at low tide, where an obligatory game of cricket often adds to the sense of occasion.

Opposite page & above Two views of Walmer Castle from the gardens.

The castle consists of four bastions with a circular centre core, and was one of a series of forts built by Henry VIII to protect ships riding at anchor in the Downs. In the eighteenth century the castle was converted into the official residence of the Lord Warden of the Cinque Ports, who have included William Pitt, Sir Winston Churchill and Her Majesty Queen Elizabeth the Queen Mother. The Lord Warden most associated with the castle is the 1st Duke of Wellington, who died in it in 1852, and visitors can see the room in which his body lay in state for two months before his funeral at St Paul's Cathedral.

The photograph on the left is of the Broad Walk, whilst that above is of The Queen Mother's Garden, planted in 1990 to mark the ninetieth birthday of the present Lord Warden, Her Majesty Queen Elizabeth the Queen Mother. The garden was designed by Penelope Hobhouse and converted from a walled kitchen garden. Amongst its plants are Californian poppies, salvias, lilies and clematis interwoven with Her Majesty's favourite scented roses.

Above A frosty morning at the church of St Nicholas, Ringwould, near Deal. The stunning cupola, or 'Kentish onion', and tower date from the seventeenth century, and their design was probably brought to this part of the county by Protestant refugees from the Low Countries.

Above Dover Eastern Docks from the clifftop, with two ferries leaving and one loading. The little white building at the end of the eastern arm of the breakwater is the Port Control Building, from where all shipping movements in and out of the Harbour are controlled.

The granite-faced breakwaters protecting the Eastern Docks were started in 1897, helping complete what is now an artificial deep-water harbour of about 700 acres. The first drive-on, drive-off ferry service at Dover was launched in 1953, before which all cars and lorries had to be crane-loaded on and off ship. The roll-on, roll-off freight service started in 1965, and despite the opening of the Channel Tunnel Dover today handles 1.7 million lorries a year, or 5,000 a day. The port's statistics are extraordinary: approximately 1,500 cross-Channel ferries berth in Dover a year, carrying 18 million passengers and 3 million cars.

Opposite page The White Cliffs of Dover. Remarkably, Dame Vera Lynn's most famous wartime song, 'There'll be bluebirds over the white cliffs of Dover', was written by an American who never actually visited them! The 400 feet high cliffs are amongst the most familiar of all English images, both to travellers landing at Dover and to those on board shipping in the Channel. What is less well-known is that the cliffs are honeycombed with tunnels dug over the centuries to defend the south coast against invasion. Five miles of this area of coastline is now the property of the National Trust, and the thin downland turf is a refuge for some of the rarest chalk-loving flowers and butterflies.

Above The Pharos, Dover, the surviving one of a pair of first century beacons built by the Romans to guide their ships into the harbour below. One of the tallest surviving structures of its period, the octagonal top was a medieval addition. Tucked in its lee is the Saxon church of St Mary-in-Castro, and for a while the Pharos served as the church's bell-tower. Eleven hundred years after the beacon was first built both buildings were enclosed by the outer fortifications of the Norman castle.

Left Dover Castle, showing the strength of its outer defences. Built within an Iron Age hillfort, Dover Castle is the most impenetrable Norman castle in England. The present keep and inner curtain wall were the work of Henry II in the twelfth century, since when it has been added to and strengthened by successive monarchs and government departments, and the castle was only finally handed over by the Ministry of Defence in 1958. The medieval underground defences were much extended during the Napoleonic Wars, when an ingenious system of remote-controlled doors was installed to trap would-be attackers. St John's Chapel, hidden in the thickness of the keep wall, is surely the most atmospheric of any castle chapel. In a field behind the castle is a memorial commemorating the first cross-Channel flight by Louis Bleriot, who landed here in 1909.

Shakespeare Cliff, between Dover and Folkestone.
The point where the Channel Tunnel goes under
the sea, Shakespeare Cliff owes its name to the
scene in *King Lear* where the blind Gloucester
meets his son Edgar, who in turn describes the
fishermen on the beach below as seeming no
bigger than mice, whilst 'The crows and choughs
that wing the midway air, Show scarce so gross as
beetles.' It is also the home of Kent's newest
landmass, a nature reserve called Samphire Hoe,
built out into the sea using spoil from the Channel
Tunnel workings.

Above Enjoying the band on The Leas, Folkestone. What was once a down-at-heel village dependent on smuggling and fishing grew slowly into a seaside resort. The arrival of the railway and a cross-Channel packet service in 1843 was one contribution, another was the laying out of much of the resort by its major landowner, the Earl of Radnor. The earl employed the architect Decimus Burton, whose idea it was to lay out the promenades, winding paths and gardens that give The Leas and the upper town their character. The bandstand dates to 1895, and has been rather unkindly described by John Newman as ' a flimsy piece of confectionery'. Below The Leas is the magnificent Leas Cliff Hall, built into the cliff-face with views out to sea.

Above The cliff lift at Folkestone links The Leas with the beach and is still powered by water, which fills tanks under the carriages on a counter-balance system. The lift dates from 1885 and is one of a handful of water-driven lifts to survive: there were once three along The Leas.

Le Shuttle trains leave the Cheriton terminal near Folkestone 24 hours a day and the service can be increased to meet demand. The advent of 'turn up and go' travel to the Continent has changed the ways by which Kent has to cope with its through traffic. A bonus to many Kent residents who regularly shop – or even work – across the Channel, its downside has been a marked increase in the number of lorries passing through the county en route for the 35 minute journey to Sangatte.

A permanent Channel link was first proposed in 1802, although digging did not start until 1880. Two World Wars and a succession of financial problems led to many false starts, and it wasn't until 1990 that engineers 'broke' through and 1994 that Her Majesty the Queen and President Mitterand of France officially opened the tunnel.

Galloping towards the finishing post at Westenhanger Racecourse, near Folkestone, Kent's only race course, which hosts a short but popular season of meetings.

HYTHE AND ROMNEY MARSH

HYTHE AND ROMNEY MARSH

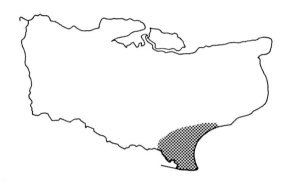

THE Romney Marshes – for there are several areas of marshland in this part of Kent – are in a class of their own. Reclaimed from the sea during the Roman period and the Middle Ages to produce the richest agricultural land in Kent they are never crowded and frequently deserted. Their isolated villages, undistinguished apart from their famous churches, have a sleepy feel about them. Built to house shepherds and agricultural labourers they lack architectural pretension. Their gardens are either clipped into perfection or overgrown and unkempt. There is nothing middle of the road about the marsh. Except the driving. The narrow lanes, often separated from the enormous fields by only a water-filled dyke, twist back on themselves. Many follow the 'innings', or plots reclaimed from the sea in successive campaigns to provide monastic houses elsewhere in Kent with an income. The few isolated houses – and there are no major houses on these marshes – are frequently to be found hidden behind tall poplars and thick hedges planted to shield them from the worst of the winds.

Travelling on the marsh is not easy. Bisected in the north-west by the Ashford to Hastings railway and crossed by the A259 southern coast road, one would have thought that its lack of contours would have made it one of the easiest parts of Kent to explore. But you will soon learn the truth. There are few direct roads. One cross-roads in the middle of nowhere leads to another. Not a house, a pub or a signpost punctuate the skyline. In spring and autumn the low mist spreads its threads across the levels, accentuating the few areas that rise above the monotonous flatlands. In early summer the croak of the marsh frog and the song of the skylark break the silence, whilst winter's snow blows into deep drifts wherever it meets a tree or fence.

The marsh is separated from the mainland by the Royal Military Canal - a rather ineffective piece of early nineteenth century engineering. Today it helps drain the marsh, much of which is below sea level. Flooding is no longer the problem it was and, indeed, some environmentalists argue that too much water is now being pumped out of the marshland to the detriment of wildlife. In the south-east corner of the marsh is Dungeness, itself a former island, an area without soil and in which nature seems to be at war with itself. Plants manage to find a footing where man cannot, and the wilderness of gravel and beach changes with each new season. Man has tried hard to tame the elements with wooden shacks, lighthouses, the not so welcome Nuclear Power Station. It is even home to a few hardy souls. But it is a far cry from the intimate downland valleys and flint-land villages that are more typical of Kent. It is another world with its own way of life.

There are two main towns, Lydd and New Romney, whilst the major shopping centre

Previous page The Romney, or Kent sheep, has long been bred on the Marsh, to cope with both the wind and the wet and boggy conditions. More sheep to the acre can be fattened on the best of the grazing grounds than anywhere else in England, and the wealthy stock farmers were once called 'Romney Kings'. Some of the old shepherds' huts with chimneys at one end and a tiled roof still survive. William Cobbett saw the sheep when on a 'Rural Ride' across the Marsh in 1823. 'The faces of these sheep are white,' he wrote, 'and indeed the whole sheep is as white as a piece of writing paper.'

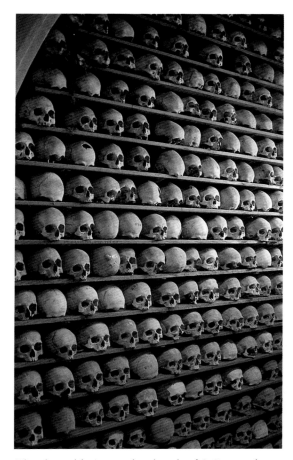

at the north-east corner of the marsh is Hythe. The latter was once a busy port, but coastal movement has left it high and dry. Not even its administrative links with Sandgate and Folkestone can recreate its character as a coastal town. It is a Maidstone on the hillside, a town with no distinct character, but much of interest if you know where to look.

The flavour of the Cinque Ports Confederation may be savoured on the marsh. This medieval grouping of five ports and two ancient towns, whose purpose was to provide ship service for the Crown in return for certain tax concessions, is all pervading. Four of the original towns were in Kent – Sandwich, Dover, Hythe and New Romney.

The Cinque Ports Confederation frequently convened their courts at New Romney, adding to its prestige. The town once supported three churches and two monastic houses, even retaining its importance after the sea had retreated in the mid-thirteenth century. The arms of the Cinque Ports may be found all over the town as indeed, they can be found across the marsh.

The charnel house at the church of St Leonard, Hythe. The ossuary in Hythe's parish church is one of only two still surviving in England. The present church was built in the thirteenth century, when the Cinque Ports were at their most prosperous, and the ossuary is housed in a medieval processional passage beneath the chancel. In the Middle Ages, when churchyard space was at a premium, it was common to clear the ground every few generations. It was not usually possible to save the remains that had been dug up, but here at Hythe this processional passage was an ideal space in which to store the skulls and larger bones. The ossuary has been open to public view for two hundred years and must rank as one of Kent's oldest tourist attractions.

Above Fishing boats on the beach at Hythe. Although Hythe lost its port during the later Middle Ages as shingle piled up from the west, and the town is now a mile inland, it still has a small fishing fleet whose boats are dragged onto the shore. The Martello towers in the background were part of a defensive chain built along the south coast during the Napoleonic Wars. Their name, and shape, stem from Mortella Point in Corsica, where a similar tower was stormed with difficulty by the British in 1794. Each of the 74 Martello towers housed a small garrison, with storage and sleeping quarters, whilst the roof gave excellent all-round sightlines. They were backed up by other fortifications, including the Royal Military Canal. Both the forts and the canal were the idea of William Pitt, who as Prime Minister was also Lord Warden of the Cinque Ports.

Lympne Castle from below. Perched on the clifftop and overlooking the remains of the Roman fort of *Portus Lemanis*, the castle was built on the site of an earlier fortification in the mid fourteenth century as a home for the archdeacons of Canterbury. Later archdeacons preferred to lease the castle as a source of income to maintain their own estates, and the last archdeacon to hold the property died in 1860. As a stone built hall house, Lympne Castle is rare in east Kent. There are extensive views over the marshes below, especially from the rather unexpected Second World War observation post on the east tower, preserved as a monument of the twentieth century's contribution to the castle's history.

Looking out over Romney Marsh from Lympne. The straggling village of Lympne stands high above the north-eastern edge of the Marsh. The area in the foreground is Romney Marsh proper, whilst in the distance it merges into Walland Marsh, one of the more recent areas to be reclaimed from the sea.

Left Appledore's thirteenth century church owes its lopsided appearance to the French, who gutted it in a raid of 1380. It contains some interesting twentieth century glass, including a window depicting local benefactor Sir William Horne with his house and chapel in the background. Horne's Place Chapel lies to the north of the village and can be visited in summer.

Because it clings to the edge of the Weald, thus trying to combine the roles of Wealden village with that of gateway to the marshes, Appledore is unlike any other Kent village. Until the 'Great Storm' of 1286 it was a busy port on the bank of the River Rother, but the shingle bank created by the storm changed the course of the river, making it run south of the Isle of Oxney. Appledore began to decline, but its charms still endure. The broad grass verges in the wide main street frame a delightful run of houses, many of them seventeenth and eighteenth century.

Right Romney Marsh in stained glass. A window in Appledore church, showing the neighbouring church of Fairfield.

Left Springtime at Snave, known locally as the 'Daffodil Church'. The church is redundant, like many on Romney Marsh, which even in the Middle Ages was over-endowed with places of worship.

Opposite page There can be few places as evocative of the Marsh as the tiny isolated church of Fairfield. There is no road to it and it never served a village, for it stands in the heart of the Marsh surrounded by a few scattered farms. A church was recorded here in the Middle Ages, and though encased in brick in the eighteenth century it was almost derelict when it was restored by W.D. Caroe in 1913. Until intensive draining of the Marsh in the last century the church was frequently cut off by floodwater, emphasising the almost imperceptible rise in the ground which left the building high and dry – though vicar and congregation once arrived by boat! The simple interior is crammed with box pews, whilst its walls are hung with text boards – a local characteristic. The church is unusual in that it lacks a churchyard, tombstones, trees or flowers.

Opposite page The Norman church of St Mary in the Marsh, whose well-cared for interior, flooded with light, is much loved by the small local community. The author Edith Nesbit (1858-1924) who wrote *The Borrowers* and *The Railway Children* is buried in the churchyard, and her grave is marked by a replica of the original wooden graveboard carved by her husband. Graveboards were once common on the Marsh, as suitable stone was rare and had to be brought in.

Right Old Romney Church once served a small port at the point where the River Rother joined the sea, and stands above the flood level on a low artificial mound. Like many coastal churches, it is dedicated to St Clement, a second century martyr who was lashed to an anchor and drowned (he is often depicted holding an anchor, and is also the patron saint of what is now Trinity House).

The lower photograph shows the interior, with its box pews, oval eighteenth century text boards and Royal Arms of George III. Cobbett visited the church on the same 'Rural Ride' as he described the Romney sheep, noting that whilst the then government was alarmed at the increase in population, Old Romney church was 'fit to contain one thousand five hundred people' , despite there being only 23 houses nearby.

An abandoned pillbox guards the Royal Military Canal, which skirts the northern edge of Romney Marsh below the escarpment. The canal runs for over 23 miles, from Hythe to west of Rye, and was dug as a second line of defence against Napoleonic invasion. It was defended by cannon and small forts that would be reached from inland behind an earth bank formed when the canal was excavated. These emplacements were set at small 'kinks' in the canal's route, which is why it does not run in a straight line. It was also intended to be used to flood the Marsh if the French successfully stormed the Martello towers on the coast, thus hampering their advance. Work started in 1803 when invasion seemed imminent, but by the date of its completion, at a cost of £230,000, the risk had passed – though it remained garrisoned until 1842.

Another of its benefits was transportation, and though a packet-boat ran on it for some years, and it was still used for carrying road-making materials at the end of the nineteenth century, an ambitious plan to link it to the Midlands canal network came to nothing. Today it is of more practical use than at any time in its history, both for its amenity value and as a way of draining the Marsh to improve arable farming. It is also a haven for wildlife, including the ubiquitous Marsh Frog; is pleasantly uncommercialised; and a waymarked footpath allows walkers to explore its entire length.

Opened in 1927 as 'The World's Smallest Public Railway', the Romney, Hythe and Dymchurch was the creation of two men, Count Zbrowski and Captain J. Howey, and remains a triumph of miniature engineering. They hoped that freight traffic would support the line but it soon became obvious that income from holidaymakers would provide the bulk of the revenue. During the Second World War the line was used by the military to transport troops and supplies along England's front line, and even an armoured train was introduced! The line runs the fourteen miles from Hythe to Dungeness, taking just over an hour. The rolling stock comprises 11 steam engines and 2 diesel locomotives, and the photograph shows the 1925 'Northern Chief' in her livery of British Railway green.

The garden of Prospect Cottage at Dungeness. The wide, wild and bleak expanses of Romney Marsh seem hardly the place for a garden, yet here amongst the fishermen's cottages and within earshot of the rocky beach, the film-maker Derek Jarman created an eerie, sculptural garden that defies the salt winds blowing in off the sea, and the doubts of the local gardeners who told him that so exposed a garden would never flourish. By introducing driftwood and scrap metal from old boats hauled up on the beach, and by grading the pebbles and shingle, Derek Jarman created a piece of sculpture in its own right that also provided hidden nooks and crannies to shelter tender seedlings. He collected stones with holes through them, which he then placed on the top of upright lengths of timber, giving a height to the garden that would have been impossible with plants alone. It is almost as if the garden had evolved naturally from its inhospitable surroundings, proving that there is more than human life and its detritus in this evocative corner of the county. Derek Jarman died in 1994 and is buried in Old Romney churchyard, where a slate slab incised with his signature marks his grave.

Above The Romney, Hythe and Dymchurch Railway curves round to its station in this view from the top of the lighthouse, whilst the houses and shacks that form the fishing community can be seen scattered across the shingle. Until recently locals tied short planks of wood to the soles of their shoes to make it easier to walk over this inhospitable terrain. Dungeness is also home to a famous RSPB reserve, as the area is often the first stop for migrant birds after their flight across the Channel – although the power lines from the Nuclear Power Station are a constant hazard.

The new lighthouse at Dungeness from the top of its predecessor, which is open to the public and provides a wonderful view over the lunar-like landscape that is Dungeness. The new lighthouse is the fifth to guide shipping round Dungeness, for unusually the coastal headland is growing rather than being eroded by the sea.

CANTERBURY AND
THE GARDEN OF ENGLAND

CANTERBURY AND
THE GARDEN OF ENGLAND

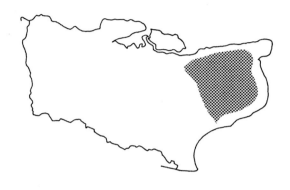

CANTERBURY stands in the valley of the Stour. Its townscape is mirrored in many a provincial English city, yet its history and sense of place in the story of England are beyond compare. More than a market town, more than a regional centre, Canterbury still reflects its former status as the seat of kings. The kings of Kent had in turn replaced the Romans, evidence of whose occupation may be found in the mosaic flooring now tucked away under the modern shopping centre. Kent's royal family established Canterbury as the centre for Christianity in England. Reminders of the city's pre-eminence are self-evident: the magnificent cathedral, its parish churches, monastic remains and half-forgotten medieval hospitals. It is a city to explore on foot and at leisure. Away from the main streets tiny public gardens, shady churchyards and echoing alleyways speak of a city that grew to serve its resident population as much as its wealth-bringing visitor. Today its university, built high on the hills overlooking the city, gives Canterbury a vibrancy by night that by day is provided by the many visitors who crowd its narrow streets.

If those self-same visitors spent a few hours exploring the countryside around Canterbury they would discover a microcosm of Kentish history. The fertile soils and north-facing slopes have long lent themselves to hop farming, market gardening and fruit orchards. Its valleys conceal picturesque villages, ancient mills and even more ancient churches. It is a countryside of narrow lanes, open skies and birdsong.

The villages to the south of Canterbury, in the valley of the River Stour, are grouped around Ashford. Once a bustling market town, few places in Kent have been so cruelly treated by the last two centuries. The nineteenth transformed it into a railway town; the mid-twentieth brought urban expansion. Now it has been reborn. The International Station has created a new hub around which Ashford continues to spawn estates.

To the east of Canterbury, the farming communities on the thin downland soils succumbed to industrialisation in the early twentieth century with the arrival of the coal industry. Villages grew rapidly to house workers brought from other parts of Britain. The landscape took on a new character, with winding wheels, conveyors and slag heaps contrasting with the open countryside and wide views. But the boom was short-lived, and it is now almost impossible to believe the impact the collieries had on the area.

One of the most beautiful parts of this area is the Elham Valley. The tiny villages with their flint churches and brick cottages enjoy a remote atmosphere punctuated only by the former market town of Elham, and the straggling village of Lyminge, which grew up around a Saxon monastery. The railway which ran up the valley has long gone. Today the area relies heavily on visitors willing to abandon the main roads in search of a 'real' Kent of bed and breakfast establishments and country inns.

Previous page Cox apples. Despite its susceptibility to scab and mildew, the Cox's Orange Pippin is widely grown in the orchards which fill the sheltered valleys around Canterbury, and is deservedly the most popular of all English dessert apples, both for its flavour and keeping qualities. The Cox was first raised near Slough from a pip of a Ribston Pippin by a retired Victorian brewer – a Mr Cox – and the original tree is said to have blown down in a gale in 1911.

Above Canterbury Cathedral viewed from the University of Kent. Canterbury is the historic administrative centre of Kent, although Maidstone is now the seat of local government. Its network of narrow streets and alleys converging on the Cathedral is well-preserved, although it struggles to cope with the volume of modern tourists. In many ways this view of the Cathedral, taken from the University founded in 1962, shows more of the majesty of the building than if it were seen from the city, where buildings crowd in on every angle. Sailing like a ship across the rooftops, the magnificent spiritual home of the Anglican Communion dwarfs almost everything else in view.

Right The south wall of St Martin's Church, Canterbury. Although not the prettiest church in the city, St Martin's is the most historic, for it is the oldest English parish church in continuous use. Its recorded history takes us back to 597, the year St Augustine arrived to convert the Saxons and found Bertha, wife of Ethelbert, Kent's king, worshipping on this spot. St Augustine baptized Ethelbert, who granted the missionary St Martin's, and Canterbury's future as the cradle of English Christianity was assured. What is less certain is whether Bertha built the church, or re-used a Roman ruin, for there are many Roman tiles to be seen in its walls. Now a thriving church with a ministry to the many pilgrims who find their way from the city centre, St Martin's is also the burial place of the writer Mary Tourtel (1874-1948) creator of Rupert Bear!

Above Canterbury Cathedral from the north west. The 235 feet tall central tower – known as 'Bell Harry', and named after a medieval bell – was one of the last parts of the cathedral to be finished in 1498. Although it looks as if completely built of stone, the top storey is of brick faced with stone, so as to match the rest of the Cathedral.

Canterbury Cathedral is one of the great masterpieces of English architecture. It was started by Archbishop Lanfranc shortly after the Norman Conquest, but belongs to no one period, so that part of its appeal is the way in which Norman, Gothic and Tudor styles are united in one building.

Right The tomb of the Black Prince, eldest son of Edward III, who died in 1376. The 'noble prince' of the battlefield, the victor at Poitiers and Crecy, married late, aged thirty-one, choosing as his bride the twice-married Joan of Kent, the 'fair maid of Kent', after whose blue riband, dropped at a ball, the Order of the Garter was named. Worn out by war, he died in his palace at Kennington when still only forty-six. That autumn he was buried on the south side of the Trinity Chapel. On his tomb rests his armour-clad effigy, helmet open, hands joined in prayer, his dog at his feet, whilst above the canopy are reminders of the uniform he wore

for so much of his life, his surcoat and gauntlets, shield and sword.

Above right A corner of the cathedral crypt. The shadow on the column is often called 'Becket's ghost' – though mundanely the shadow is the

result of the crypt once being used as a coal store. The twelfth century crypt is the largest Norman crypt in Europe, and part is still used by the descendants of Canterbury's French Huguenot community, who were originally allowed to worship in it in late Tudor times.

Right Canterbury Cathedral's towering late fourteenth century nave, seen from the east. The late Middle Ages were not always kind to the Cathedral. Archbishop Sudbury, one of its most prolific builders and responsible for starting the nave, was murdered during the Peasants Revolt of 1381, and an earthquake struck the city the following year.

Recently, the foundations of an earlier, Saxon, church were found beneath the nave floor, indicating that the local tradition of the Cathedral being founded on this exact spot by St Augustine, may be based on the truth.

Below The Corona, a rounded eastern addition to the Cathedral built in the late twelfth century to house a small shrine to St Thomas à Becket, which was used in conjunction with the main shrine in the adjacent Trinity Chapel. The murder in the Cathedral of Thomas à Becket in 1170, whilst Archbishop and at the instigation of Henry II, is one of the great dramatic moments in the Cathedral's history. He was canonised two years later, and the trickle of pilgrims already visiting Canterbury turned into a flood, enriching both city and cathedral.

Above Christmas shopping in Canterbury. Those who know the city well can lead you to an array of small specialist shops tucked away in the back streets, where old-fashioned goods and welcoming service provide a contrast to those aimed principally at the tourist.

Above Westgate Towers, Canterbury. Always a floral spectacular, the small municipal gardens on the banks of the River Stour can get crowded with visitors. The river actually divides just before it reaches the city, so may be seen in several different places within its walls. The heavily fortified Westgate, built simultaneously with the city walls in the late fourteenth century of grey Kentish Ragstone, provides a good rooftop view of the Cathedral, and it is within its shadow that visiting monarchs are offered the keys to the city.

A mass of bluebells just outside Canterbury. Bluebells are a familiar spring flower of the Kent countryside, and are seen at their best in woodland which has been coppiced eighteen months earlier, allowing in light.

Coppicing, or the practice of regularly cutting down woodland so as to provide a continuous supply of timber and underwood, was at its peak when the iron industry in the Weald demanded vast amounts of charcoal. Multi-stemmed trees are still a familiar sight in Kent woods, particularly of sweet chestnut, oak, ash and alder, all of which provided slender poles ideal for charcoal burning. As the iron industry collapsed during the seventeenth century, coppiced wood became popular for fencing and a whole range of other uses in rural communities, from supports for the wire-work in the hop gardens to chair-bodging.

England's smallest town hall: Fordwich. The village was the inland port for medieval Canterbury. Situated at the highest navigable point on the River Stour its quayside was much used to take materials and goods to the city. Its function as a port also lead to its acceptance as a member of the Cinque Ports Confederation, whose arms are to be found on the village sign. The Tudor Town Hall had a storeroom and prison on the ground floor and court room above. Originally the timbers were separated by plaster panels, but in the seventeenth century bricks were substituted and a pleasant herringbone effect was the result. Time has been kind to Fordwich. The weedy Stour is deep and fast-flowing. The village is full of houses of character and an atmospheric, though redundant church, providing a great contrast to Canterbury's bustling centre.

A fisherman at Grove Ferry near Canterbury. A pretty spot on the River Stour from where boat trips through tall reedbeds may be taken in the summer.

Above Ickham Barns. Filling one side of the village green in front of Ickham Church, this magnificent run of farm buildings is a reminder that the wealth that built these village churches was firmly rooted in the area's agriculture. The church, which dates in the main from the thirteenth century contains two medieval effigies.

Below 'Waterfall Cottage', Patrixbourne, which was once an estate village for Bifrons, the long-demolished seat of Marquess Conyngham. The cottage owes its name to its magnificent water gardens, a series of interlocking ponds and lakes once part of the pleasure gardens for Bifrons House.

Below The fruits of Kent's gardens and orchards piled at the foot of the font for Harvest Festival in St Mary, Patrixbourne. A Norman church, with a glorious Norman door under the tower, it contains a remarkable collection of Swiss stained glass, all of it enamelled and much of it set against an alpine background.

The eighteenth century Littlebourne House, and a row of small seventeenth century brick cottages in the village of Littlebourne. Brick was an early arrival in this part of Kent, partly because of a lack of good quality local stone, and partly due to the influence of settlers from the Low Countries.

Sparks flying at Nailbourne Forge. The craftsmanship of Julian Coode and Martin Reeves is well-known throughout Kent. Much of their work is connected with the restoration of period ironwork, but they also produce startling contemporary designs for objects as diverse as candlesticks, street furniture and large scale screens. The iron industry of medieval Kent was confined to the Weald, but improvements in transport and communication have given the traditional industries freedom to move in search of new markets.

Top Court Farm, a lovely old farmhouse dating back to the fifteenth century in the small hamlet of Leaveland.

Right A thatcher at work in the village of St Nicholas at Wade. The village takes its name from the medieval travellers who waded across the Wantsum Channel, which once divided the Isle of Thanet from the rest of Kent. Medieval maps show people being carried across the mudflats at low tide, and it is probable that those same mudflats originally provided reed for thatching the houses here. Thatched roofs are not common in Kent, where clay for tiles was always close at hand, but most villages on the edge of the marshy areas boast a handful of thatched cottages.

Opposite page The classic Kent view: orchards and oasthouses near Selling.

Right At work and at rest in the hop gardens. The fact that hops in Kent are grown in gardens, not fields, is supposedly the outcome of evading a medieval tax on any crop grown commercially. The man in the tractor bucket is cutting down the bines, after which they are loaded into carts and taken to the picking machine, usually in a shed, where mechanical flails strip the hops from the bine.

The mechanisation of the hop industry has destroyed a way of life. Until the 1960s thousands of Londoners annually descended on Kent in late summer on board special trains to pick the hop harvest. Lines of small single storey huts were built for the pickers, whose Cockney rhyming slang and cheerful good humour gave the hop gardens a character all of their own. It was a working holiday, enjoyed on the same farm year after year, and punctuated in the evenings by campfire sing songs and a little discreet poaching. Many hoppers even settled in Kent, an influx whose accents can still be heard in hop-growing areas.

Above The view from Elham church tower. The quiet Elham Valley offers a taste of unspoiled Kent. The Square at Elham, dominated on one side by the parish church, presents a domestic feel in its architecture. Not too grand to impose its character, yet slightly too retiring for its own good, it offers a welcome alternative in a county that is better known for its village greens than market squares.

Left An unexpected sight in the 'Garden of England' – a field of ripe pumpkins ready for Hallowe'en at Barham Downs.

Above Chilham's Victorian flour mill on the banks of the River Stour is considered to be the best preserved in southern England, and its mostly timber machinery is still kept in perfect working order. It originally ran six pairs of grinding stones, finally closing in 1934, when the mill was sold and its millstream turned into watercress beds. The mill building now houses pumping equipment for the local water supply.

Right Chillenden post mill. Despite their rarity, the advantage of a post mill over a smock mill can easily be seen, as the whole building can be turned to face the wind. Chillenden's is a wonderful example, and was built in 1868 to grind both corn and cattle feed. The unspoiled and rather lovely village of Chillenden sits in the shadow of its more famous neighbour, Goodnestone.

Above A distant view of Wingham to the east of Canterbury. The old centre of the village huddles around a dog-leg turn in the main road, and its wide main street hints at wealthier times. The parish church of St Mary, which formerly supported a college of priests, is large and airy, although the wooden piers in the south arcade suggest that the wealth was short-lived. In fact, the money collected for building a new nave after the Reformation was embezzled by a local brewer, and the parish could only afford wood. This is the Kent of popular imagination, with a mixture of arable, fruit and livestock farming filling the relatively flat landscapes between Canterbury and Deal.

Left The south side of Barfrestone church. In a county where Norman work invariably means heavy, solid masonry, Barfrestone (or 'Barson' as it is sometimes known locally), is a pure delight. The exuberance of the stone-carving on the outside of this tiny church is unequalled by any other building of a similar date in the country. The church of St Nicholas is thought to have been paid for by one generous donor in the late twelfth century, and was built of local flint and Caen stone shipped from across the Channel. The south doorway, seen here, contains a multitude of images, ranging from Christ in Majesty to the four evangelists and a veritable host of angels. There are animal musicians, the signs of the Zodiac and the Labours of the Months. The corbel table, whose lines of heads run around the church below the eaves, is particularly exciting, with all sorts of mythical faces peering down on the visitor.

Goodnestone Park. The village of Goodnestone (pronounced 'Gunston' to distinguish it from another village in Kent of the same name), is one of the prettiest estate villages in the county. Its Victorian cottages and rebuilt church were built and paid for by the Bridges family, who have lived at Goodnestone Park for over 250 years. The red brick house was built in 1704 by Sir Brook Bridges, an official in the late Stuart Treasury. Today it is the home of his descendant, Lord FitzWalter. The gardens surrounding the house have recently been restored and extended by the present Lady FitzWalter and are open to the public. Woodland walks and herbaceous borders have been laid out and planted to compliment the architecture of the house and adjacent church.

Goodnestone Park was well-known to Jane Austen, who refers to it in many of her letters. Her eldest brother, Edward, married Elizabeth Bridges, and the couple lived at Godmersham, only a few miles to the west. Jane spent the summer of 1796 staying nearby, and wrote of attending a ball at the house with Edward and dancing country dances, afterwards walking home 'at night under the shade of two umbrellas'.

Chilham Castle from the south. The present red brick mansion was built in the early seventeenth century by Sir Dudley Digges to replace an unusual multi-angular Norman keep which still stands nearby. The gardens, which have views down into the Stour Valley, include the first wisteria to be planted in the country. Chilham Castle is one of the few buildings to dominate the narrow valley of the River Stour.

Recently restored to its original eighteenth century glory, Godmersham Park was the home of Jane Austen's brother, Edward (see also Goodnestone on the previous page). The magnificent park surrounding the house is occasionally open, attracting devotees of Jane Austen, who see its influence in many of her novels, most particularly *Mansfield Park*.

The photograph below shows the River Stour flowing through the park.

MAIDSTONE AND THE WEALD

MAIDSTONE AND THE WEALD

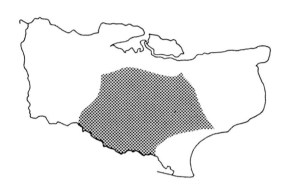

MAIDSTONE is the usurper of Canterbury's crown. Its more central location has given it the administrative edge, and for two hundred years it has been the county town. Not that it is lacking in character. But much of its architecture dates to the last thirty years, particularly in the centre where new buildings dominate the Medway and what remains of the historic core: imagine what the riverside might have been like with townhouses and moorings, lawns and walks. Small corners still exude charm – around the Archbishop's Palace and in Brenchley Gardens for example – but Maidstone's biggest asset is Mote Park, the former seat of the Earls of Romney, 650 acres just ten minutes walk from the town centre, and which is now part sportsground, part nature reserve, and part woodland and lake.

The surrounding villages often appear to be more picturesque than they really are, but nearly all hide a quiet corner or pleasant surprise. They are working villages, rooted in farming, which improve the further they are from London. The edge of the Greensand

Previous page Collecting conkers from the chestnuts in Headcorn churchyard.

The Archbishop's Palace in a secluded backwater on the bank of the River Medway at Maidstone was a popular overnight stop for medieval Archbishops on their journey from Canterbury to London, replacing their less convenient palace at Wrotham. The former stable block houses one of the finest collections of horse-drawn carriages in the world, bequeathed to the town by a former mayor, whilst the main building is home to the town's Register Office, a café and function suite. In recent years, an annual River Festival has filled these normally quiet moorings with gaily decorated boats.

Ridge is the only dramatic topographical feature, and once in the Weald it is the buildings that give character and interest. Villages that were once remote are increasingly accessible. They still, however, offer many delights: the narrow lane that leads to an old mill, a group of abandoned oast houses that the developer has yet to discover, the roadside stall whose honesty box bulges on purely local trade.

The central Weald, south of the Greensand Ridge, was inaccessible in winter until the nineteenth century, its heavy clay soil churning into a quagmire and making wheeled transport almost impossible. Once roads were driven through, followed later by the railway, the character of this part of Kent changed for good. The former market centres declined as people travelled to Maidstone, Tonbridge or Ashford, but luckily those that survived without widespread mid-nineteenth century expansion remain largely unspoilt. Goudhurst, Cranbrook and Tenterden are very much alive and characterful, even though the car which maintains their economy detracts from their visual appeal.

It is easy to forget that the Weald covers an enormous area and is not confined to Kent – the larger portion runs west across Sussex and Surrey into Hampshire. Its boundaries have long been difficult to define: as early as 1576 Kent's first historian, William Lambarde, wrote of the need for a 'verdite of twelve men' to determine it. Geologically, it covers the area between the two great rims of chalk that form the North and South Downs, although the Greensand Ridge near Maidstone is frequently taken as its northern edge. Until the nineteenth century tithes payable on Wealden woodland were less than outside it, leading to boundary disputes from parishes eager to be included.

It is hard to imagine the large forests that flourished here until the late Middle Ages. Only here and there are there remnants of the ancient, managed woodlands that provided timber for houses, ships and charcoal. The Weald has changed and continues to do so. Like much of Kent it is a working environment where a balance between 'olde' English cosiness and the harsh reality of twenty-first century commerce has to be made.

Above This unusual early Gothic Methodist church in Union Street, Maidstone, dates from the early nineteenth century.

A Shire horse pulling a brewer's dray during a display at the County Showground, just outside Maidstone. The Showground is host to a succession of events throughout the year, but is still best known for the County Agricultural Show in July.

Left Rural Kent at its most idyllic. Blue skies, and cricket on Bearsted's village green.

Below left Stoneacre. Otham is rich in medieval houses, but only Stoneacre is open to the public. It was built in about 1480 as a yeoman's hall house, and remodelled in Tudor times, later declining in status from manor to farmhouse and gradually falling into disrepair. Early in the twentieth century it was bought by the architectural historian, Aymer Vallance, who both restored and enlarged it using authentic medieval materials salvaged from redundant buildings before presenting it to the National Trust.

Opposite page Two views of Leeds Castle: at dawn, and with hot-air balloons rising over the battlements.

   One of Kent's most picturesque historic houses, Leeds Castle stands on an island in a lake formed by the River Len. Saxon fragments still survive, though it was enlarged after the Norman Conquest and the present building is predominantly late medieval. As well as being home to six English queens, it was where both Richard II and Joan of Navarre, Henry IV's widow, were imprisoned. The castle passed from the Crown in 1542, first becoming a Tudor courtesan's house and then the home of the Culpeper (or Colepepper) family. The castle is more visually exciting from the outside, for the interiors are a strange mixture of medieval and twentieth century fashion. It was saved from possible dereliction in the 1920s by the Hon Lady Baillie, and remained her home until her death in 1974.

Left The Loose stream. The village of Loose, now almost a suburb of Maidstone, sits in a deep valley carved by the stream that shares its name (probably *leose*, the Old English for pigsty). It is hard to believe that this was once a major industrial centre, the stream providing power to over a dozen paper and fulling mills, many of which remain – though most have been converted into private houses. The village was bypassed in 1829 by the construction of a road viaduct designed by Thomas Telford, and Maidstone's suburbs have yet to trespass on the steep hills and cluster of roofs that give the village such charm.

Below Aylesford village from the new bridge. Aylesford's fourteenth century ragstone bridge is now closed to traffic, creating a peaceful vantage point from which to view the village. Although medieval ferries plied to and fro across the Medway, Aylesford was the only permanent crossing place between Maidstone and Rochester, making it the heart of this part of the Medway valley until Maidstone overshadowed it. The majority of the riverside houses shown here are nineteenth century, although the large white house in the foreground was once a prosperous inn, and provided the setting for the opening scene of the film of 'Half a Sixpence' (1966).

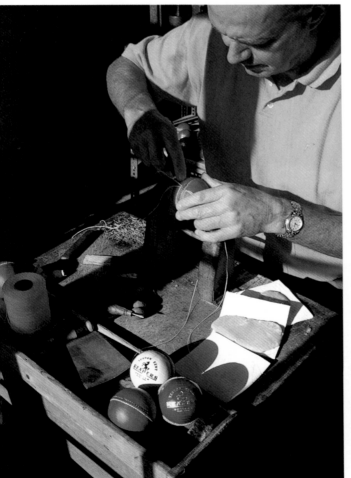

Left Stitching cricket balls at A. Reader & Co. Ltd., Teston. Cricket ball and bat manufacturers were once common in West Kent, but like many such trades there are just a handful of surviving works. Cricket balls are still made in Teston, a few miles west of Maidstone, as they have been for over 140 years and where staff at Alfred Reader's still hand-stitch them in the traditional fashion.

A busy afternoon at Teston bridge. One of several medieval bridges to cross the Medway, Teston bridge has the familiar pedestrian refuges or projections built onto its piers.

Boxley church from the south west. The tiny village of Boxley stands just below the Pilgrims' Way to the north of Maidstone, beside the high speed rail link to the Channel Tunnel. The church sits at the end of a narrow village green and is actually two churches in one, a medieval nave and chancel being added on the end of a Norman nave and chancel, which was then heightened to become this tower. One of the finest sections of the Pilgrims Way runs along the left hand side of this view, with banked woodland above its northern flank and open farmland to the south.

A watermill at Westwell. The village owes its name to the many springs in the area, whilst a grant of 1296 in Canterbury Cathedral Library mentions Westwell's mills. Two centuries later the miller's grandson fell into a millpond at Westwell, to be saved by a passing pilgrim praying to Henry VI, then popularly regarded as a saint: the boy floated still alive to the surface and was revived.

St Mary's Church and Lake House, Eastwell. The ruins of St Mary's Church stand in the grounds of Eastwell Manor, which is now a hotel, and are maintained by The Friends of Friendless Churches. Tradition says that Richard Plantagenet, illegitimate son of Richard III (reigned 1483-1485) is buried beside the forty acre lake, having fled to Kent following the death of his father at the Battle of Bosworth. He is supposed to have become a labourer on the estate, eventually living in the house to the right of the church, and the site of his grave is now marked by a simple chest-tomb. The church fell into disrepair after the Second World War following the collapse of its roof. There was never a village at Eastwell, the church being regarded as more of a manorial chapel than a parish church.

Eurostar trains at Ashford International Station. Rising majestically over the low-rise buildings in the centre of Ashford, the International Station is the late twentieth century's most important contribution to the town. The opening of the Channel Tunnel in 1994 has revived Ashford's fortunes, with new out-of-town retail and commercial developments opening almost monthly.

Steaming along with the Kent and East Sussex Railway. This preserved light railway runs 10 miles from Tenterden to Bodiam through the rolling countryside along the Kent/Sussex border. The railway only reached Tenterden in 1900 as a small branch line, and a later link with the main line at Headcorn had little impact on the town. Passenger services were withdrawn after only half a century and in 1961 part of the line south of Tenterden was taken over by a preservation society.

Right Headcorn churchyard and village. Headcorn is a bustling one-street village between Sutton Valence and Biddenden. The surrounding landscape may be a little flat, but that is more than compensated for by the wealth of domestic and ecclesiastical architecture in the village, which includes tile-hanging, weatherboarding and black-and-white timberwork. Many of the buildings betray the influence of the Flemish weavers who once settled in the village, adding to its medieval reputation for cloth-making.

The pest house in the churchyard of Great Chart church. The pest house stands on a high hill looking towards Ashford, but its name is misleading. Whilst local tradition asserts that plague victims were housed in it so that their fellow parishioners could pray for their souls, it was more likely to have been a 'Priest's House', providing overnight accommodation for a chantry priest. Chantry priests were paid to pray for individual benefactors, travelling from one church to another on a regular basis, and were often housed in small cottages near the church.

The Black Horse pub, Pluckley, in the heart of the Weald. The inn is now internationally renowned as 'Pop' Larkin's local in the television series taken from H.E. Bates's *The Darling Buds of May*. The round-headed windows are a local feature, traditionally installed in all properties owned by the Dering estate after a member of the family escaped from a similarly-shaped window whilst being held prisoner during the Civil War.

Looking down from the tower at Sissinghurst Castle on a fragment of what are probably the most influential gardens created in Britain during the twentieth century (and the most photographed). Sissinghurst's gardens were the creation of the writer Vita Sackville-West (1892-1962) and her husband, the politician Harold Nicholson (1886-1968), who bought the remains of the Tudor castle and its surrounding buildings in 1930. Gradually, over a period of years, they laid out a series of themed outdoor 'rooms', Sir Harold doing most of the designing, whilst his wife did the planting. The Castle and its gardens now belong to the National Trust.

The Cottage Garden, Sissinghurst Castle. The climbing rose is 'Madame Alfred Carrière', the first flower to be planted by the Nicholsons after buying the house.

Left Cranbrook and its windmill. The 70 feet high Union Mill of 1814 is the largest smock mill in England and dominates the upper end of the town. It takes its name from a group – or union – of creditors that took it over when its first owner went bankrupt. It is well-cared for and in full working order.

Cranbrook is yet another example of a cloth town, whose produce was exported to the Low Countries until a law of 1566 forbade this lucrative trade. When Elizabeth I visited Cranbrook she is reputed to have walked down a mile long piece of broadcloth. The town has a magnificent church, which includes an unusual baptistry in which adults being baptised were totally immersed, whilst its many medieval timber-framed buildings include a branch of Lloyds Bank!

Below Tenterden High Street. The transition from market town to tourist town has done little to spoil Tenterden's charms. Iron and cloth made it rich, and it was once allied to the Cinque Ports, with a dock at Smallhythe.

Like Smarden, Tenterden could easily be an architectural guide to Kentish building styles, and this photograph alone shows weatherboarding blending happily with tile-hanging and bow-fronted windows.

Below Biddenden village. The footpaths in the High Street of this delightful village are paved with local Bethersden marble, a form of limestone rich in shell fossils. Although the marble can be found throughout the Weald, Biddenden is the best place to see it. Like many villages in the Weald, Biddenden's prosperity was founded on the cloth trade: the first floor windows on the house in the foreground once lit long weavers' workshops. The Red Lion Inn was supposedly built by a soldier after returning from the Battle of Agincourt in 1415, whilst All Saints Church has a fifteenth century tower built of a different, unpolished form of Bethersden marble.

Smallhythe Place, an evocative fifteenth century house that was the home of the actress Ellen Terry (1847-1928) for the last thirty years of her life. Smallhythe was originally a small port and shipyard on a tributary of the Rother. Until the draining of the levels in the last century fairly sizeable boats could navigate what is now little more than a ditch at the bottom of the garden. Smallhythe Place is thought to have been the harbourmaster's house. It now contains a wonderfully eclectic collection of theatrical memorabilia, including many of Ellen Terry's costumes and stage props, and there is a small barn theatre in the gardens.

The Booth Motor Museum at Rolvenden. An unusual private museum to find in a small Wealden village, the C.M. Booth Museum of Historic Vehicles contains ten three-wheeled Morgan cars dating from 1913-1935 and the only known example of a Humber Tri-car of 1904. These are parked within an outstanding display of model and toy cars, road signs, and motorcycles.

Rolvenden smock mill. The eighteenth century mill stands prominently on high ground along the road towards Cranbrook. It worked until the turn of the twentieth century, and was finally superbly restored in 1957 by Mr. and Mrs. Harold Barham of Hole Park in memory of their teenage son, tragically killed in a road accident.

Below Pattyndenne Manor, Goudhurst. The Kentish hall house is the jewel in its architectural crown. Most were built by the now extinct breed of yeoman farmer at a time when Kent was by far England's wealthiest county. 'A Yeoman of Kent,' went a rhyme, 'With his yearly rent,' could buy out a knight, a nobleman and a laird.

The typical hall house began as a central hall open to a timber roof, with the hearth in the centre. There was a two-storeyed wing at either end, one wing providing the farmer and his family with a parlour and a master bedroom, the other containing domestic quarters and bedrooms for servants and children. With time, the fireplace was moved to one end of the hall. Pattyndenne dates from 1470 and is double-jettied, in that the first floor projects on all four sides. The close studding, or the use of vertical timbers to create a wall that is substantially more timber than plaster, was a sign of wealth, though it became rarer as the local supply of timber began to fail.

Pattyndenne owes its name to the Old English for a 'stream quick to flood'. The heavy clay soils of the Weald cause such a run-off that the stream bordering Pattyndenne's garden can still rise feet in minutes after heavy rain. The house was a hunting lodge during the reign of Henry VIII, who is supposed to have visited it, becoming a working farm shortly afterwards.

Above One of the highest villages in the Weald (at 406 feet), and marred by twenty-first century traffic, Goudhurst is still worthy of a visit, if only to admire the view from the churchyard over the surrounding hop gardens and Bedgebury Pinetum. Goudhurst, like several other Wealden villages and towns, was at its most prosperous when it was a centre for iron smelting and weaving.

The lake at Bedgebury Pinetum. The spectacular 65 acre garden contains the most comprehensive collection of conifers in Europe. It was first established by the politician Alexander Beresford-Hope who lived at Bedgebury Park in the mid-nineteenth century. The house may be glimpsed from the woodland walks and is now a well-known school. The Pinetum, which is open throughout the year, is managed by the Forestry Commission and runs a popular education programme.

Storm clouds gathering over Wye Crown. Wye Downs, facing south towards Ashford, afford splendid views over the valley of the Stour and towards the Weald of Kent. The crown was cut into the chalk to mark the coronation of Edward VII in 1902.

Scotney Castle, near Lamberhurst, was built as a fortified manor house in 1378 by Roger Ashburnham as a defensive measure against the French. Massive engineering was required to employ the River Bewl and its tributary the Sweetbourne to the greatest possible effect, although the castle's position at the foot of a valley gave it little strategic importance.

For nearly 400 years the castle was home to the Catholic Darell family, who almost ruined themselves refacing it in the classical style in the seventeenth century. The castle was later sold to the Husseys, a family of rich ironmasters, who in 1837 began building a new 'castle' on the hill overlooking the old, which was then turned into a picturesque ruin. Following the death of the writer and architectural historian Christopher Hussey in 1970 the castle and its gardens were acquired by the National Trust.

Rhododendron Dell, Scotney Castle. The gardens are famed for their balance of deciduous and evergreen trees and shrubs, creating glorious seasonal contrasts. Stone for the Victorian house was quarried locally, and its abandoned workings provide a dramatic landscape feature.

TUNBRIDGE WELLS
AND THE WEST

TUNBRIDGE WELLS
AND THE WEST

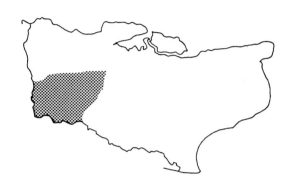

THIS is the Kent beloved by visitors – of picturesque countryside, tea shops, stately houses and gardens. Add to that a heady mixture of Winston Churchill, James Wolfe, Sir Philip Sidney and Beau Nash and you find a microcosm of English history. Half-timbered yeoman's houses on the edge of the Weald rub shoulders with historic castles set within a landscape that belongs far from London and the motorways that cut through Kent's leafy lanes.

Tunbridge Wells could stand alongside the commuter territory of Petts Wood and Dunton Green as a newcomer to the Kent landscape. The only difference being that it was new four hundred years ago instead of one hundred and fifty. The historic centres of Sevenoaks and Tonbridge, both established on dry rising ground, have in turn given birth to new suburbs, but only Tunbridge Wells has exceeded its parent in size and achievement. It is unique in Kent as having been established as a spa in the early seventeenth century. Its proximity to London and the ease with which it became part of the social scene meant that it soon attracted many visitors. Such was the social demand for easy access to 'the Wells', as they are known locally, the first turnpike in the county was built to serve it rather than the more commercially attractive Channel ports. However, the dense Wealden forests into which Tunbridge Wells pushed its

Previous page Roses and thatch cover a cottage in Yalding.

Groombridge Place is approached from beside the village green, but the house itself is well-hidden in a valley. It was built of local red brick in the seventeenth century to replace an earlier moated manor, and is still a private home.

embryonic fingers remained a formidable barrier until the nineteenth century.

The upper reaches of west Kent are served by the River Darent, although the villages in its valley make little use of its waters. The more southern areas are lucky enough to have the River Medway and its tributary, the Beult, meandering through their hop gardens and orchards. But again there are few riverside villages, most preferring to sit on high ground above a valley notorious for its floods until only recently.

The northern Holmesdale Valley, with its feet firmly bedded beneath the overpowering North Downs, and whose villages formed the edge of the medieval Wealden forest, ends in a more gentle north-facing slope that runs up the Greensand Ridge. This area has much woodland, dotted by grand nineteenth century houses enjoying even grander views over the upper Medway Valley. Few medieval settlers penetrated the area, which is rich in wildlife and offers numerous walks. What north-south roads there are usually began life as roads for the drovers who led their livestock up from the verdant valley to the London markets.

As the escarpment drops away to the valley floor we find denser populations around Tonbridge and Tunbridge Wells. Be sure never to confuse them – residents of each have a sense of civic pride unrivalled in Kent and, after all, there is still a narrow greenbelt between the two! Sitting uncomfortably, and somewhat aloof, within that greenbelt is Bidborough, where the sandstone ridge rises sharply to create a panoramic viewpoint facing north-west. From here the Medway Valley appears to be wide and flat, although in reality it is punctuated by small rises on which stand its villages and is criss-crossed by the streams and ditches that feed the Medway. This is the Kent of country estates; Penshurst, Hever, Chartwell, Squerryes. The villages continue to prosper and there is still work for the traditional craftsman. Almost every turn in the road brings with it a change in character, for nothing holds these villages together. Each is a testament to its own development and the devotion that successive residents have given to preserving their surroundings.

Above Eddie Hare – nose to beak – with Helga the Bald Eagle. The Raptor Centre at Groombridge provides both an important sanctuary and also a rescue service and breeding centre for birds of prey. A large aviary shelters eagles, hawks, falcons, owls and vultures.

A corner of one of the herbaceous borders at Groombridge Place. Unusually for a garden, those at Groombridge Place can be reached via the Spa Valley Steam Railway, which runs from Tunbridge Wells. Despite having opened to the public relatively recently the gardens are already immensely popular.

Sir Arthur Conan Doyle, the creator of Sherlock Holmes, found Groombridge's extraordinary yew topiary so menacing he incorporated it into his novel *The Valley of Fear*. Conan Doyle lived locally at Crowborough and there is a reconstruction of his study at Groombridge Place.

Above 'The Pantiles' in Tunbridge Wells (which gained the prefix 'Royal' in 1909) provide one of those views that is instantly recognisable. They were laid out in 1638 as a fashionable walk on which to be seen after taking the waters. Tunbridge Wells is a seventeenth century creation and it is lucky to have kept its most famous feature more or less intact. The present colonnaded buildings replaced booths and stalls selling local produce to visitors, a function many continue to perform, albeit on a grander scale. The name 'pantile' derives from the earthenware tiles given to the town by Queen Anne to pave the Walks, and of which all but 15 were later replaced with flagstones.

It is said that Queen Anne's generosity was due to her frail son, the Duke of Gloucester, tripping on the uneven surface of the Upper Walk. When the Queen next returned and found the work not even started she became so incensed she vowed never to visit the town again.

Left Taking the waters at Tunbridge Wells. The town owes its fame to Lord North, who became lost returning to London in 1606 and instead found a chalybeate, or iron-bearing, spring, whose waters once drank speeded his recovery from consumption. Because Tunbridge Wells was closer to London than its main rival, Bath, it quickly became fashionable. The spa's reputation was further helped by the arrival of Charles I's queen, Henrietta Maria, and her son, the future Charles II. Their patronage lead to the town's rapid expansion and the building of large town houses on the slopes above the spring. Mount Ephraim and Mount Sion were the two most popular residential locations, taking their names from the prevailing Puritan atmosphere of seventeenth century Kent.

The waters may still be taken from the springs in front of the former Bath House whilst a visitor attraction, 'A Day at the Wells', shows what life was like in the town during its most fashionable heyday. The water collects from an underground spring into a marble basin, and is poured into a small tumbler by the resident 'dipper', who is officially appointed by the Lord of the Manor of Rusthall. Although it is a well-attested fact that the first 'dipper', Mrs Humphreys (whom the actress is impersonating here) lived to be 102, no one seriously lays claim to any positive medicinal benefit of the water today.

Right The elaborate coat-of-arms (of the Duchess of Kent, Queen Victoria's mother) on the portico outside the Rose and Crown Hotel in Tonbridge High Street hark back to an age when it was an important coaching inn on the London–Tunbridge Wells road, the first in the county to be turnpiked.

Below The east window of All Saints, Tudeley. The church at Tudeley, described in the 1790s as of 'little interest', today contains 12 stained glass windows by the Russian artist Marc Chagall, whose work is widely regarded as some of the most exceptional stained glass of the twentieth century. The east window was commissioned by Sir Henry and Lady d'Avigdor Goldsmid as a memorial to their daughter, Sarah, who drowned whilst sailing in 1963. Sarah can be seen about to be lifted up to Heaven from the swirling waters, watched over by Christ on the Cross. Chagall finally filled every window in this isolated church with his stained glass, the last of them being installed in the year of his death, 1985.

Below The thirteenth century gatehouse to Tonbridge Castle from the lawn. Kent's best example of a motte and bailey castle was originally built to protect a vulnerable crossing point on the upper reaches of the Medway. Its muddled ownership is one of intrigue and violent death, occasionally from an executioner's axe. The castle was partly demolished in 1793 when it was bought by Thomas Hooker, who built the Gothic house on the right (now used as a council office and an award winning Tourist Information Centre). The gatehouse's soft honey-coloured sandstone is typical of this part of Kent, and is open to the public.

Opposite page Penshurst Place. The top photograph shows the north front from the cricket pitch in the Deer Park. *Bottom right* is of the Great Hall, round which the present house evolved, and which was built in about 1340 by Sir John de Pulteney, four times London's Lord Mayor. In Tudor times it passed to the Sidney family, who still own it today. For a while it was almost a ruin, but later generations of the family gradually restored and rebuilt it. The family has long been distinguished, and include the 1st Viscount de L'Isle, V.C., who died in 1991, and Sir Philip Sidney (1554-1586), the Elizabethan poet and soldier who died from his wounds whilst fighting in Holland aged thirty-one, and who offered his water flask to another dying soldier with the words 'your need is greater than mine.' The third photograph is of a corner of the gardens.

Right Hever Castle. The castle is most famous as the childhood home of the doomed Anne Boleyn, who as Henry VIII's second wife ultimately paid with her life for failing to bear him a son. In 1903 it was bought by the American financier William Waldorf Astor, who spent ten million dollars restoring and enlarging the house and creating gardens to house his collection of antique statuary. 1,500 labourers spent four years diverting the course of the River Eden to form the lake, a new drawbridge was built, as was a mock Tudor village to house his guests. Amongst Hever's treasures is the prayer book carried by Anne Boleyn to her execution. The castle was sold by the Astors in 1983 although they still live locally. The castle is open daily throughout the summer and the new water maze (*below*) is popular with children.

Fallow deer grazing the Deer Park at Knole, with a corner of the house just visible on the skyline. The 1,000 acre park is nationally recognized for its fungi and lichens, whilst the house's 365 rooms, 52 staircases and 7 courtyards – as well as replicating the calendar – reputedly make it the largest private house in the country, described by Vita Sackville-West, who was born in it, as 'a town rather than a house'. It was given to Thomas Sackville, Lord High Treasurer, by his cousin Elizabeth I in 1566, although he did not take possession of the property until the early seventeenth century. Though the house now belongs to the National Trust the family continue to live there and own the park.

Six Bells Lane, Sevenoaks: a cluster of weather-boarded cottages on the steep lane that skirts the church. The passage takes its name from an earlier peal of bells which was melted down in the eighteenth century and recast with additional metal to produce the present peal of eight. Though not a stone's throw from the bustling High Street, the lane is quite simply the prettiest in Kent.

Ightham Mote is reached down a wooded lane near the hamlet of Ivy Hatch. The medieval moated house was built in a narrow valley called Dinas Dene, and was occupied by a succession of families who held minor positions of importance before being restored and given to the National Trust by an American, Charles Henry Robinson, who died in 1985. Built of local ragstone with oak timber-framing, the house grew slowly, with successive owners gradually completing another of its four sides. Even the entrance spans two phases, the base dating from its medieval construction whilst the top was rebuilt later in brick. Much of Ightham Mote's charm lies in its interior, which is small and homely.

A sea of ripening corn fringes Trottiscliffe church: the name comes from the steep escarpment to the north of the village, though it is pronounced 'Trosley' – the form of spelling being gradually adopted. The parish church and site of a former palace of the Bishops of Rochester stand in a hollow some distance from the modern village. It is overlooked by the Pilgrims Way, whose route follows the treeline at the base of the far hill. The church contains box pews and an outstanding eighteenth century pulpit which originally stood in Westminster Abbey, complete with sounding board supported by a wooden palm tree. The artist Graham Sutherland (1903-1986) is buried in the churchyard.

The Coldrum Stones, near Trottiscliffe, frame a view of the Medway Valley. Kent has two major centres of neolithic settlement, both on high ground near the Pilgrims Way overlooking the Medway Valley. The Coldrum Stones are all that survives of a burial chamber, in which were found human remains dating to the late Stone Age (about 2,500 BC).

Chartwell, near Westerham, will always be associated with the private family life of Sir Winston Churchill (1874-1965), specially the period during the 1920s and 30s when his political fortunes were at their lowest. He wrote that here he 'never had a dull or idle moment from morning to midnight' so engaged was he on gardening and painting in this sheltered valley. It was bought by a group of Churchill's friends in 1946 and presented to the National Trust, and is now very much a place of pilgrimage.

The brooding familiar figure of Sir Winston Churchill, a detail from the statue by Oscar Nemon on Westerham Green. Churchill bought Chartwell to the south of the village in 1922 and lived there until his death in 1965. The bronze shows him reclining in an armchair.

Quebec House, Westerham. The home of General James Wolfe (1727-1759) for the first eleven years of his life, Quebec House (in his days known as Spiers) is a square brick and ragstone house which dates from the sixteenth century. It is now cared for by the National Trust and contains a small collection of pictures of Wolfe and some of his personal possessions including his snuffbox and dressing gown.

Below James Wolfe died whilst leading the attack on the French town of Quebec, and his bronze statue, with sword raised is at the other end of the village green to Churchill's more famous statue.

Squerryes Court, Westerham. The fine William and Mary house has been the home of the Warde family since 1731. George Warde was a great friend of the Wolfe family and it was on a visit to Squerryes that James Wolfe received his first commission. The house is still very much a family home whose rooms evoke the character of a well-to-do country gentleman's residence of the eighteenth and nineteenth centuries. The lakes in the grounds are the source of the River Darent, which joins the Thames near Dartford.

Brasted village green, with its pump beneath a chestnut tree and a row of tile-hung cottages. Thanks to the M25 and the attractions of neighbouring Westerham it still retains a little of its character. England's oldest firm of builders, Durtnells, established in 1591, are based in the village, and the White Hart Inn has a memorial to the Battle of Britain pilots from nearby Biggin Hill.

The only surviving quintain in the country stands on Offham's village green. Tilting-posts such as this were once common, mainly as a sport for village lads, though their origins date back to medieval times when they provided a form of 'target practice' for knights and mounted soldiers. The cross-bar swivels, so that the weighted end hit a rider on the back if his horse was too slow or he was badly positioned.

The High Street, Wrotham, a delightful and still thriving village just south of the Pilgrims Way. It owes its medieval prosperity to a palace of the Archbishops of Canterbury that stood until the end of the fourteenth century. The parish church dominates the village, although this view shows the main street, many of whose houses take their names from the shops and trades that once occupied them. Several major industries are based on the local clay, including Wrotham Ware – a form of slipware pottery still made in the village.

Walkers on the Pilgrims Way. The Pilgrims Way is a late Victorian invention coined to provide a suitable name for a long distance footpath that runs from Canterbury along the Downs escarpment, leaving the county near Westerham. Despite its name, the way is far older than Christianity, and was originally a prehistoric track running from the Isle of Thanet to the West Country. Many muddle it with Watling Street, mistaking it for the route followed by Chaucer's pilgrims in *The Canterbury Tales*. Although much has been tarmaced, some sections still pass through open country – as here, between Wrotham and Kemsing, with the Vale of Holmesdale and the Medway Valley in the distance. It follows the firmer ground above the spring line, rarely passing through a village, so modern walkers can happily drop down into a nearby village for a welcoming drink and a meal.

ACKNOWLEDGEMENTS

Beltring Hop Farm. Whilst Kent is dotted with oast houses for drying hops, the world's largest single grouping is at Beltring, near Paddock Wood. They were originally owned by Whitbread, and now form part of a Country Park, with displays on hop farming and paddocks grazed by the Shire horses that originally pulled the brewery drays.

A large number of people have helped in the creation of this book, and our thanks are due to them all. First and foremost, there are the people of Kent who by chance appear in the photographs, either wittingly or unwittingly. Then there are those, listed below, who have generously helped by providing facilities for photography not normally available. Our principal regret is that lack of space has meant that we have only been able to include a fraction of the photographs.

A particular debt is owed to the booksellers throughout Kent who have encouraged the project: without their support it would never have been started. More specifically our thanks must also go to the following for their generous help and assistance: Viscount De L'Isle for his permission to photograph Penshurst Place; Leeds Castle Foundation for allowing us to photograph the balloon festival; the Dean and Chapter of Canterbury Cathedral for granting permission to photograph inside the Cathedral; English Heritage; The National Trust; The Churches Conservation Trust and The Friends of Friendless Churches.

We are also grateful for assistance with information or permission to photograph to Stephen Alexander; Audrey Barber; Julian Berry; Barbara Budworth; Richard and Katrina Burnett; Gordon and Joy Clarkson; Douglas Chapman (Dode Church); Mother Concordia; Julian Coode; Rod Cooper; Bob Crane; Betty Cripps; Paul and Alison Davis; Colin Dawson (Dreamland); Dover Harbour Board;   Mike and Suzanne Edmeades-Stearns (Nurstead Court); David Evans Silk Mill; Claudia Fisher; Delia Fitt; Lord and Lady FitzWalter; Caroline Foster; Candy Francis; Doreen Gilham; Rev. Gary Gill; Carol Gofton; the late Edward Hollamby; Shaun Hughes; Michael Ivatt; Jocelyn Kennard; David Kenward; Sheila Kostyrka (Tonbridge and Malling Borough Council); Colin Mann; Sally Mewson-Hyndes; Rod and Hilary Martin; Camille Newall (Eurotunnel, Folkestone); Mrs Angela Prior (on behalf of the Dean and Chapter of Canterbury Cathedral); Alfred Reader and Co. Ltd.; Rev. Christopher Reed; Martin Reeves; Rev. Canon Jonathan Russell; Ken Scott; Corrine Scutt; David Spearing (Pattyndenne Manor); Jill Stanners; Margaret Taylor; Joan Tovey; Tracy Turner; Bonnie Vernon; Tracey Wahdan; Michael Wheatley-Ward (Theatre Royal, Margate); John and Anthea Warde; Lizzie Warren; Angela Youngs.

GREGORY HOLYOAKE AND JOHN E. VIGAR

INDEX

Appledore 68
Ashford 101
Aylesford 98

Barfrestone 90
Barham Downs 88
Bearsted 96
Beckenham 14
Bedgebury Pinetum 109
Beltring 126
Bexley 14
Bexleyheath 15
Biddenden 105
Bleak House 47
Bluewater 12
Botany Bay 46
Boxley 99
Brands Hatch 18
Brasted 123
Broadstairs 47
Bromley 12

Canterbury 77, 78, 79, 80, 81
Canterbury Cathedral 77, 78, 79
Capel-le-Ferne 49
Chartwell 121
Chatham 25, 30
Chilham 89, 91
Chillenden 89
Chinese Garage 14
Cobham 16, 17
Cobham Hall 16
Cooling 21
Cooling Castle 20
Cranbrook 105
Crayford 14
Cray, River 14

Darent, River 19
Deal 52
Dode Church 21
Dover 56, 57, 58, 59
Dover Castle 59

Down House 13
Dungeness 73, 74

Eastwell 100
Elham 88
Eltham Palace 13
Eynsford 19

Fairfield 69
Farningham 19
Faversham 36, 37, 38
Folkestone 39, 61, 62
Fordwich 82

Godmersham Park 92
Goodnestone Park 91
Goodwin Sands 53
Goudhurst 108
Gravesend 9, 18
Great Chart Church 102
Groombridge Place 112, 113
Grove Ferry 82

Hall Place 14
Harty 32
Headcorn 93, 102
Herne Bay 43
Hever Castle 117
Hythe 65

Ickham 83
Ightham Mote 119
Ivy Hatch 120

Kingsferry Bridge 31
Knole 118

Lamberhurst 110
Leather Bottle 16
Leaveland 85
Leeds Castle 97
Le Shuttle 62
Littlebourne 84

Loose 98
Lullingstone 19
Lympne Castle 66

Maidstone 94, 95
Margate 44, 45
Medway Bridge 25
Medway, River 22, 25, 94
Minster 50

Nailbourne 84
Newington 32
Newnham 34
North Foreland Lighthouse 46
Nurstead 17
Nurstead Court 17

Oare Marshes 35
Offham 124
Old Romney 71
Otham 96
Owletts 17

Patrixbourne 83
Penshurst Place 116
Pilgrims Way 125
Pluckley 103
Queenborough 31
Queen Elizabeth II Bridge 11

Ramsgate 48
Reculver 44
Red House 15
Richborough Castle 50
Ringwold 55
Rochester 27, 28, 29
Rochester Castle 26, 29
Rolvenden 107
Romney Marsh, Frontispiece, 63, 67,
    68, 69, 70, 71, 72, 73
Royal Military Canal 72

Sandwich 51

Sarre 1
Scotney Castle 110, 128
Selling 86
Sevenoaks 118
Shakespeare Cliff 60
Sissinghurst Castle 104
Sittingbourne 34
Smallhythe Place 106
Smarden 4
Snave 68
Squerryes Court 123
Stalisfield 33
St Mary in the Marsh 70
St Nicholas at Wade 85
Stoneacre 96
Stour, River 82, 92
Swale, River 23
Swanscombe 10

Tenterden 105
Teston 98, 99
Teynham 33
Thames, River 10, 11, 18
Tolhurst Farm 4
Tonbridge 115
Tonbridge Castle 115
Trottiscliffe 120
Tudeley 115
Tunbridge Wells 114

Upnor 22
Viking Bay 47

Walmer Castle 54, 55
Westenhanger Racecourse 62
Westerham 121, 122, 123
Westgate Towers 80
Westwell 100
Whitstable 40, 41, 42, 43
Wingham 90
Wrotham 124
Wye Downs 109
Yalding 111

The boat house, Scotney Castle